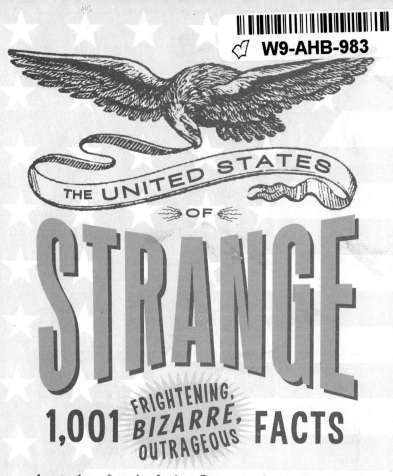

THE UNITED STATES

OF

STRANGE

1,001 *FRIGHTENING, BIZARRE, OUTRAGEOUS* **FACTS**

about the Land of the Free and the Home of
**THE FROG PEOPLE, THE COCKROACH
HALL OF FAME, AND CARHENGE**

ERIC GRZYMKOWSKI

▲**adams**media
Avon, Massachusetts

Published by
Adams Media, a division of F+W Media, Inc.
57 Littlefield Street, Avon, MA 02322. U.S.A.
www.adamsmedia.com

ISBN 10: 1-4405-3614-7
ISBN 13: 978-1-4405-3614-4
eISBN 10: 1-4405-3620-1
eISBN 13: 978-1-4405-3620-5

Printed in the United States of America.

10   9   8   7   6   5   4

This publication is designed to provide accurate and authoritative information with regard to the subject matter covered. It is sold with the understanding that the publisher is not engaged in rendering legal, accounting, or other professional advice. If legal advice or other expert assistance is required, the services of a competent professional person should be sought.

—From a *Declaration of Principles* jointly adopted by a Committee of the American Bar Association and a Committee of Publishers and Associations

Many of the designations used by manufacturers and sellers to distinguish their product are claimed as trademarks. Where those designations appear in this book and Adams Media was aware of a trademark claim, the designations have been printed with initial capital letters.

Certain sections of this book deal with activities and devices that would be in violation of various federal, state, and local laws if actually carried out or constructed. We do not advocate the breaking of any law. This information is for entertainment purposes only. We recommend that you contact your local law enforcement officials before undertaking any project based upon any information obtained from this book. We are not responsible for, nor do we assume any liability for, damages resulting from the use of any information in this book.

Interior illustrations © clipart.com; Pg. 44 istockphoto/DavidBukach; Pg. 46 istockphoto/fractalgr; Pg. 66 istockphoto/ultra_generic; Pg. 129 pills istockphoto/tokhiti.

CONTENTS

Introduction . . . 5

DEDICATION

To my Godmother Linda, who instilled in me an immense love of facts and refused to let me win when we played Trivial Pursuit.

ACKNOWLEDGMENTS

Most authors wait until the end to thank their readers for their generous patronage, but I prefer to start the butt-kissing at the bottom and work my way up. So thank you, dear reader, for selecting this humble tome to grace your coffee table or bathroom magazine basket. I do truly hope you enjoy it.

Of course, dear reader, if it were not for my editor Peter Archer and all the folks at Adams Media, you might never have the pleasure of learning about the New York City "Mole People." The Adams staff continually impress me with the quality of their creations, and I am grateful to have the chance to work with them yet again.

And lastly, I would like to thank all the countless journalists, authors, bloggers, and fact gurus who made it possible for me to compile this tome. Your dedication to the pursuit of weird knowledge is truly awe-inspiring.

INTRODUCTION

We like to think that America is the epitome of normal. An entire nation of blue jeans, family-friendly minivans, and weekend barbecues. Sure we may indulge in the occasional deep-fried stick of butter, but for the most part nothing strange or out of the ordinary ever happens in the good ol' U.S. of A. But deep down we all know this couldn't be further from the truth.

In reality, America may very well be the weirdest place on earth. Which is pretty impressive, considering the competition from places like North Korea, Outer Mongolia, and France.

Through countless hours of research, I managed to uncover everything from a museum in Maryland devoted entirely to feminine hygiene products to a six-foot-tall man eating chicken in New York City (the hyphen placement is important there). And that was just the tip of the iceberg.

No matter where you are in this country, you are just a few miles from a plethora of oddities. You can indulge in jellied moose nose in Alaska or munch on deep-fried bull testicles in Colorado. You can visit haunted lighthouses, cemeteries, cruise ships, and space shuttle launch pads from coast to coast. If you should happen to find yourself in Alliance, Nebraska, there's even a scale replica of Stonehenge built out of classic American cars.

It's easy to write off these quirky tourist traps and strange delicacies as indulgences only fit for the weirdest of the weird of our countrymen, but you really are missing out on a lot if you don't give them a chance. Thankfully you don't need to crisscross the continent to experience all the strangeness this country has to offer. With this book you can do it all from the comfort of your couch (or, more likely, your toilet).

So dive right in and embrace the wonderful world of the weird. Just don't blame me if, when you've turned the last page, you're too terrified to leave your house.

CHAPTER 1

Got a Permit for That Flamethrower?

Obscure American Laws to Embrace

For the land of the free, we certainly spend a lot of time telling our citizens what they can and can't do. We are all aware of the important laws—don't drive too fast, resist the urge to strangle your neighbor—but what does the law say about hunting buffalo with a machine gun while driving down a California highway?

Some of the laws in this chapter may seem strange, obscure, or downright ridiculous, but keep in mind: There are no unnecessary laws. At some point, somewhere, somebody did something stupid enough that a new law needed to be written to determine his fate.

Due to an amendment to the Immigration
and Nationality Act (INA) passed in 1965 that
added "sexual deviation" as a medical ground for
denying prospective immigrants entry into the
United States, scores of open homosexuals were
denied entry into the country. This practice
continued until the U.S. Congress passed the
Immigration Act of 1990, which withdrew the
phrase "sexual deviation" from the INA.
*"Give me your tired, your poor, your huddled masses yearning
to breathe free. . . But please leave your gay uncle at home."*

❯ Tracy J. Davis, "Opening the Doors of Immigration: Sexual Orientation and
Asylum in the United States," American University Washington College of Law,
www.wcl.american.edu.

Due to a number of hepatitis cases
linked to tattoo parlors in New York in
1961, the city placed a ban on tattooing
that would not be lifted until thirty-six
years later in 1997. *"What am I supposed to
do? Just tell my mom I love her?"*

❯ Randy Kennedy, "Cappuccino
with Your Tattoo? Try That on
a Sailor," *The New York Times,*
July 27, 1997, *www.nytimes
.com.*

Most American children reach adulthood at the
age of eighteen, but kids in Nebraska have to wait a
little longer. The state doesn't recognize the age of
majority for residents until they reach nineteen.
*A word of advice for Nebraskan children: Stay a kid as long as
humanly possible.*

❯ Nancy Hicks, "Age of Majority in Nebraska Could Change
for Some Purposes," *Lincoln
Journal Star,* January 20, 2010,
www.journalstar.com.

Thirsty Pennsylvanians may not
purchase more than two packages of
beer at the same time, unless they do
so from a designated beer distributor.
*And now we know where Captain Buzz Killington
calls home.*

❯ "Pennsylvania," Dumblaws
.com, *www.dumblaws.com.*

Residents of Waco, Texas, are forbidden from
eating bananas and tossing the peels into the street.
Lawmakers feared horses could slip on the peels and
injure themselves. *Anyone who has ever played Mario Kart
knows you can tap B to prevent a slide out.*

❯ Sheryl Lindsell-Roberts, K. R.
Hobbie, Ted LeValliant, and Mar-
cel Theroux, *Wacky Laws, Weird
Decisions & Strange Statutes*
(Main Street, 2004), 10.

Drug dealers in Tennessee are required
to submit tax forms to account for their illicit wares.
Anonymously, of course. *Are crack pipes deductible?*

❯ "Unauthorized Substances Tax," Tennessee Government, *www.tn.gov.*

The California Board of Equalization
once ruled that bartenders in the
state could not be held responsible
for misjudging the age of midgets.
Aren't children just midgets without IDs?

❯ Bruce Felton, Mark Fowler,
*The Best, Worst, & Most
Unusual: Noteworthy Achieve-
ments, Events, Feats, &
Blunders of Every Conceivable
Kind* (Galahad, 2004), 286.

To deal with the overwhelming homeless population in New York City, the city will pay for a one-
way ticket to anywhere in the world if the individual
can verify that a relative will be there to take them
in. The program costs the city $500,000 a year.
As an alternative solution, I offered to walk the streets and yell,
"Get a job" at every bum I saw. I would only charge $50,000
a year for this service. The city disrespectfully declined.

❯ Julie Bosman, "City Aids
Homeless with One-Way Tickets
Home, *The New York Times*,
July 28, 2009, *www.nytimes*
.com.

In 1874, Albert Packer became the first man
in the United States to be convicted of cannibalism.

Well, at least he wasn't wasteful.

❯ Varla Ventura, *Book of the Bizarre: Freaky Facts and Strange Stories* (Red Wheel, 2008).

An individual who has participated in
a duel is ineligible for governorship in
Pennsylvania. *Based on what I know of the state,*
I'm surprised the opposite isn't the case.

❯ "United States Weird Laws,"
LawGuru, *www.lawguru.com*.

Facing a debt crisis in 2011, Topeka, Kansas,
took a controversial approach to saving money.
The city repealed its domestic violence laws
so citizens wouldn't have to pay for the trials.
Beats having a bake sale . . .

❯ Colleen Curry, "Topeka
Repeals Domestic Violence
Law," ABC News, October 12,
2011, *www.abcnews.go.com*.

Oregon and Louisiana do not require a unanimous guilty verdict to convict a defendant of a crime. *Because hung juries are for suckers.*

> "Jury Voting Requirements to Return a Verdict," Lawyers.com, *www.lawyers.com.*

California sheepherders are exempt from the state's hourly minimum wage laws. Instead, they must be compensated monthly at a rate no less than $1,422.52 per month. *Because it's hard to convince sheep to take care of themselves from 5:01 P.M. until 8:59 A.M.*

> "Minimum Wage," California Department of Industrial Relations, *www.dir.ca.gov/dlse/faq_minimumwage.htm.*

While it is illegal for convicted felons to vote in many states, there is **no law barring them from running for presidential office.** *Being a criminal is almost a prerequisite for the presidency.*

> Patt Morrison, "Felons Make Lineup for State's Presidential Primary," *Los Angeles Times*, January 5, 2004, *www.latimes.com.*

Despite popular opinion, Title 14, Section 1211 of the *Code of Federal Regulations* did not make it illegal for Americans to have contact with extraterrestrials or their vehicles. Instead, the law was enacted just before the *Apollo 11* mission to make it legal for the government to quarantine the astronauts should they become contaminated with an alien virus during the walk on the moon. *Bonus Fact: The law was repealed in 1991.*

❯ "E.T. Make Bail," Snopes, *www.snopes.com.*

Although women were not granted the right to vote until 1920, state laws in New Jersey allowed women to vote as early as 1776, a right they frequently exercised until 1807 when the state restricted voting to white men. *Close call. Nearly ruined the "armpit of the nation" reputation.*

❯ "Stories From the Revolution," National Park Service, *www.nps.gov.*

In November 2011, Michigan passed anti-bullying legislation that contained a controversial clause exempting disparaging remarks based on "sincerely held religious beliefs or moral conviction." The bill passed, but the clause was later removed. *But officer, it says "Johnny has bitch tits" right here in Matthew 4:7.*

❯ Marilisa Kinney Sachteleben, "Michigan House Removes 'Religion Clause' from Anti-Bullying Legislation," Yahoo! News, November 12, 2011, *www.news.yahoo.com.*

In 1998, the city of Wilson, North Carolina, outlawed the keeping of upholstered furniture on front porches, on the basis that the practice was unsightly and tacky. *Confederate flags are cool though.*

❯ Rick Bragg, "Comfort vs. Style in Town Clash on Porches," *The New York Times*, January 2, 1998, *www.nytimes.com.*

In the city of Coeur d'Alene, Idaho, a police officer who suspects the occupants of a vehicle are having sex must honk or flash his or her lights and wait for a period of three minutes before approaching the car. *Creepily eating popcorn during those three minutes is optional.*

> "Idaho," Dumblaws.com, *www.dumblaws.com*.

It is illegal to sell human breast milk for the purposes of consumption in the state of California. *Don't worry; you can still give it to friends as a gift.*

> "Health and Safety Code Section 1647–1648," Official California Legislative Information, *www.leginfo.ca.gov*.

Despite a California law requiring new car owners to obtain license plates within six months, Apple CEO Steve Jobs managed to drive around for years without them. His secret? He simply swapped his current car for a new one every six months. *Don't hate the player, hate the game.*

> Alex Heath, "Why Steve Jobs' Mercedes Never Had a License Plate," Cult of Mac, October 26, 2011, *www.cultofmac.com*.

It is illegal in certain areas of Maine to step out of a plane while it is in the air.

Fairly difficult to enforce once they're out though.

> Sheryl Lindsell-Roberts, K. R. Hobbie, Ted LeValliant, and Marcel Theroux, *Wacky Laws, Weird Decisions & Strange Statutes* (Main Street, 2004), 8.

After noticing an increasing number of students embracing in the hallways, school officials in Hillsdale, New Jersey, imposed a "three-second hugging" rule in 2009. According to them, they worried the constant displays of affection could clog hallways. *Finally, a worthy sequel to* Footloose?

❯ Sarah Kershaw, "For Teenagers, Hello Means 'How About a Hug?'" *The New York Times,* May 27, 2009, *www.nytimes.com.*

Peyote is considered an illegal substance in all fifty states. However, Native Americans are permitted to use it during religious ceremonies. *For the small price of a few centuries of oppression, you too can legally get high on peyote.*

❯ 42 U.S.C. § 1996a. "Traditional Indian Religious Use of Peyote," Cornell University Law School, *www.law.cornell.edu.*

Only ten states in the United States have laws **banning the ownership** and use of a flamethrower. *God, I love this country.*

❯ Robert Evans, "7 Items You Won't Believe Are Actually Legal," *Cracked,* February 2, 2009, *www.cracked.com.*

The penalty for eating nuts on a public bus in Charleston, South Carolina, can be as much as $500 and sixty days in jail. *Hear, hear! If you want to eat nuts, get your own goddamned bus.*

> Sheryl Lindsell-Roberts, K. R. Hobbie, Ted LeValliant, and Marcel Theroux, *Wacky Laws, Weird Decisions & Strange Statutes* (Main Street, 2004), 13.

Until 2009, there was no law

in Rhode Island preventing minors from dancing at strip clubs. *Giggity.*

> Amanda Milkovits, "Minors in R.I. Can Be Strippers," *The Providence Journal,* July 21, 2009, *www.projo.com.*

The Expatriation Act of 1907 declared that **any American woman who married a foreign national** thereby forfeited her citizenship. *His accent doesn't seem so sexy now, does it?*

> "Landmarks in Immigration History," Digital History, *www.digitalhistory.uh.edu.*

Hawaii is the only state that does not permit the sport of falconry. *How can they prove you are falconing? Perhaps an eagle just happened to land on your wrist and put a hood over its own head.*

> "Getting Started," American Falconry, *www.americanfalconry.com.*

In Kentucky, it is illegal to carry a concealed weapon that is more than six feet long. *How you might go about concealing it is anybody's guess.*

> Jan Payne, *The World's Best Book: The Spookiest, Smelliest, Wildest, Oldest, Weirdest, Brainiest, and Funniest Facts* (Running Press Kids, 2009).

The record for fastest confirmed speeding ticket belongs to Samuel Armstrong Tilley of Stillwater, Minnesota. While riding a Honda 1000 motorcycle, Tilley rocketed to 205 mph before police promptly pulled him over. *Human stupidity will always transcend limits.*

> "Minnesota Trooper Writes 205 mph Speeding Ticket," *USA Today*, September 21, 2004, www.usatoday.com.

Bearing an "obscene and indecent tattoo" can bar you from admission to the U.S. Navy.

I ♥ Mom is only offensive if you really mean it.

> Noel Botham, *The Mega Book of Useless Information* (John Blake, 2009), 261.

In the state of California, it is illegal to be in possession of "broad-tipped indelible markers" (read: permanent markers) in public. The law is in place to curb graffiti and other acts of vandalism. *Humming is permitted, but only if you do so softly on the third Tuesday of each month.*

> Cezary Jan Strusiewicz, "6 Laws You've Broken Without Even Realizing It," *Cracked*, September 26, 2011, www.cracked.com.

Due to the efforts of the Committee

to End Pay Toilets in America, Chicago banned pay toilets in 1974. *I owe the committee so much.*

❯ Bruce Felton, Mark Fowler, *The Best, Worst, & Most Unusual: Noteworthy Achievements, Events, Feats, & Blunders of Every Conceivable Kind* (Galahad, 2004), 262.

The first drug law in America was enacted in San Francisco to prohibit the use of opium in Chinese opium dens. The drug was perfectly legal everywhere else in the city. *I was unaware the danger of drugs was location based.*

❯ Jill Harness, "Little Known Facts About American History," Neatorama, February 25, 2010, *www.neatorama.com.*

When he realized how few of his fellow legislators took the time to thoroughly read proposed bills, Texas Representative Tom Moore Jr. introduced a bill honoring Albert DeSalvo (a.k.a. The Boston Strangler) for his work in population control. The resolution passed unanimously. *I'm not sure which possibility is scarier: That they didn't read it, or that they read it and agreed wholeheartedly.*

❯ Leland Gregory, *Stupid History: Tales of Stupidity, Strangeness, and Mythconceptions Throughout the Ages* (Andrews McMeel, 2007), 27.

It is illegal to cut off a chicken's head in Columbus, Georgia. But only on Sundays. *If a zombie chicken is terrorizing your family, you don't have time to check the day.*

❯ "Stupid Laws In Georgia," Stupidlaws.com, *www.stupid laws.com.*

Children working in the entertainment industry are exempt from many child labor laws. Some states will issue work papers to an infant as young as fifteen days old. *If kids don't want to work, they shouldn't eat so much.*

❯ Dane Sherwood, Sandy Wood, and Kara Kovalchik, *The Pocket Idiot's Guide to Not So Useless Facts* (Penguin Group, 2006).

In Los Angeles, California, it is illegal to poke a turkey for sale in a meat market in order to determine its degree of tenderness. *If they know a better way, I'd love to hear it.*

❯ Sheryl Lindsell-Roberts, K. R. Hobbie, Ted LeValliant, and Marcel Theroux, *Wacky Laws, Weird Decisions & Strange Statutes* (Main Street, 2004), 27.

There are currently no federal laws requiring state-run detention facilities to report the death of an inmate. *If you can't trust corrupt prison guards, who can you trust?*

❯ Hannah Levintova, "Tracking Prison Deaths Is Tougher Than You'd Think," *Mother Jones*, August 9, 2011, *www.mother jones.com*.

In 1979, pieces of NASA's *Skylab* space station landed in Australia. The United States was fined $400 for littering but never paid. *If you want the money, you'll have to come off your island and get it, Kangaroo Jack.*

❯ "The Discovernator," Discovery Channel, *www.news.discovery.com*.

Although almost universally ignored by the general population, the Metric Conversion Act of 1975 declared the metric system the preferred method for measurements in this country. *If you measure in meters, the communists win.*

❯ Sophia Dembling, "Losing the Battle By Inches," *Chicago Tribune*, October 15, 2006, www.chicagotribune.com.

Residents of Maine who live in log cabins are exempt from property tax. *In related news, woodpeckers are astonishingly difficult to kill.*

❯ Erin Barrett and Jack Mingo, *Random Kinds Of Factness: 1001 (or So) Absolutely True Tidbits About (Mostly) Everything* (Conari Press, 2005), 3.

When Montana instituted daytime speed limits on its interstate highways, the number of fatal car accidents increased by 111 percent. *Irony is a dish best served at 110 mph while text messaging and shaving.*

❯ Chad Dornsife, "Montana: No Speed Limit Safety Paradox," National Motorists Association, May 10, 2011, www.motorists.org.

It is against the law in Minnesota to hang both male and female underwear from the same drying line. *Is it still considered female underwear if I'm the one who wears it?*

❯ Pustak Mahal, *501 Astonishing Facts* (Pustak Mahal, January 30, 2010).

Sunshine is lawfully guaranteed to

the citizens of California. *It is impossible to describe how obnoxious this is.*

> Noel Botham, *The Mega Book of Useless Information* (John Blake, 2009), 245.

Individuals who pump their own gas in New Jersey face a fine of up to $250 for a first offense and $500 for subsequent offenses. *Just think of the gas station attendant as your temporary servant.*

> Cathy Pelekakis, "New Jersey Gasoline Laws," eHow, December 1, 2010, *www.ehow.com*.

Residents of Virginia are legally permitted to consume alcohol the day before their twenty-first birthday. *Just wait the extra day. Your liver will appreciate it.*

> Frequently Asked Questions, Virginia Department of Alcoholic Beverage Control, *www.abc.virginia.gov*.

Living people cannot appear on postage stamps. *It discourages mail-in campaigns, but encourages suicides.*

> Noel Botham, *The Mega Book of Useless Information* (John Blake, 2009), 261.

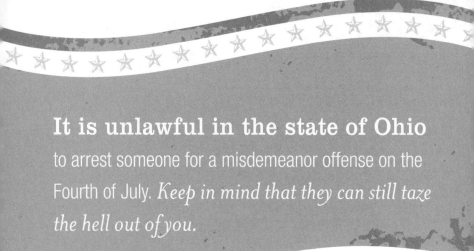

It is unlawful in the state of Ohio to arrest someone for a misdemeanor offense on the Fourth of July. *Keep in mind that they can still taze the hell out of you.*

> Tim O'Brian, "Let Freedom (and Strange July 4th Facts) Ring! Ripley's Believe It or Not! Chronicles Independence Day Oddities, Such as When the Liberty Bell 'Really' Rang For the First Time!," *Ripley's Newsroom*, June 13, 2011, *www.ripleysnewsroom.com.*

Liquor stores in Louisiana may not sell milk. *Keeps out the milk junkies.*

> "United States Weird Laws," LawGuru, *www.lawguru.com.*

Between 2006 and 2007, nearly 250,000 students were subjected to corporal punishment in public schools. *To be fair, most of them were asking for it.*

> M. J. Stephey, "Corporal Punishment in U.S. Schools," *Time,* August 12, 2009, *www.time.com.*

Although a husband or wife cannot be forced to bear witness against their spouse, there is no such law to protect siblings. As such, it is possible that one conjoined twin could be called upon to provide testimony against the other. *Kind of tough to plead ignorance there.*

❯ Daniel Engber, "If a Siamese Twin Commits Murder, Does His Brother Get Punished, Too?", *Slate*, January 5, 2010, *www .slate.com.*

Prisons in Wisconsin may not serve artificial butter to inmates.

Life behind bars is bad enough without margarine.

❯ "United States Weird Laws," LawGuru, *www.lawguru.com.*

To circumvent laws banning the sale of ice cream on Sundays, ice cream vendors in Ohio put fruit on top to disguise the frozen treat below, giving rise to the ice cream sundae. *Necessity is the mother of deliciousness.*

❯ "53 Crazy Laws," Random History, *http://facts.random history.com/.*

Until 2005, the United States banned the importation of Sichuan peppers—a small pod casing that causes numbness in the mouth—into the country. *Normally I frown on government intervention when it comes to my stomach, but I appreciate their attempt to save me from myself.*

❯ Florence Fabricant, "Sichuan's Signature Is Now Legal Again," *The New York Times*, July 27, 2005, *www.nytimes.com.*

According to the United States government, the flag represents a living country and is itself considered a living thing. *So yes, if you start sewing one and give up halfway through, that is an abortion.*

> 4 U.S.C. § 8 "Respect for Flag," Cornell University Law School, *www.law.cornell.edu.*

The only time it is permissible to fly the American flag upside down is when you are doing so to indicate you are in a state of distress. *Or when you really want to get beaten up by patriotic rednecks.*

> Steve Berges, *Founding Fathers Fun Facts: And Other U.S. Trivia* (American Liberty Press, 2010), 31.

Corporal punishment is legal in schools in twenty U.S. states. *And there's a paddling in it for anyone who objects.*

> M. J. Stephey, "Corporal Punishment in U.S. Schools," *Time*, August 12, 2009, *www.time.com.*

Before Prohibition, New York City sported 15,000 legal saloons. Before the end of Prohibition, there were more than 30,000 illegal ones. *Always bet on vice.*

> Ian Lendler, *Alcoholica Esoterica: A Collection of Useful and Useless Information As It Relates to the History and Consumption of All Manner of Booze* (Penguin, 2005). 229.

In Willowdale, Oregon, it is illegal for men to talk dirty to their wives during intercourse. *Or after.*

> "Top 10 WTF? US Sex Laws," *College Times, www.collegetimes.us.*

It is illegal to mail pornography, pork products, or any artifacts deemed objectionable to the Islamic faith to members of the U.S. military operating oversees. *Seems like there's an opening for a bacon smuggling ring if you are up to the challenge.*

> "APO/FPO/DPO Guidelines & Restrictions," United States Postal Service, *www.usps.com.*

Only thirty-two U.S. states have laws prohibiting **sex with animals**. *Land of the free indeed.*

> Jennifer Sullivan, "Enumclaw-Area Animal-Sex Case Investigated," *The Seattle Times,* July 15, 2005, *www.seattletimes.com.*

Although rarely invoked, a Frankenstein veto occurs when a governor vetoes certain words in a bill to create a new bill not previously passed by legislators. For example, Wisconsin governor Jim Doyle once condensed a 272-word passage into a twenty-word sentence that took $427 million from the transportation budget and gave it to public schools. *So Congress, please never, ever, include the words "unlimited," "monkey," and "butlers" in a single bill.*

❭ Monica Davey, "Wisconsin Voters Excise Editing From Governor's Veto Powers," *The New York Times*, April 3, 2008, *www.nytimes.com*.

It is illegal in Zion, Illinois,

to give a lit cigar to a pet. *Otherwise they'd never learn to do it themselves.*

❭ Sheila De La Rosa, *The Encyclopedia of Weird* (Torkids, 2005), 91.

It is strictly forbidden for business owners or individuals in the state of Kentucky to sell, purchase, own, or trade a duck that has been dyed blue. *So if you want to see a blue duck, you'll just have to draw your own.*

❭ "Blue Ducks—A Kentucky Law," *Stupid Laws & Dumb State Laws, www.lawsome.net.*

It is illegal to plough a field in

North Carolina with an elephant. *Or a fat person wearing an elephant costume.*

❭ Noel Botham, *The World's Greatest Book of Useless Information* (John Blake, 2005), 202.

Those caught throwing snowballs in Provo, Utah, can be subject to a fine of $50. *Remember, kids, it's not technically a snowball if there's a rock in the middle.*

❯ "Utah," Dumblaws.com, *www.dumblaws.com.*

Pedestrians in Alaska may not

intentionally avoid stepping on the cracks while walking on paved sidewalks. *Sorry, Mom.*

❯ "Stupid Laws In Alaska," Stupidlaws.com, *www.stupidlaws.com.*

Unless the target is a whale, in California it is illegal to shoot any animal from a moving vehicle. *Sweet. My bazooka enthusiasts' whale-hunting excursion is still a green light.*

❯ "United States Weird Laws," LawGuru, *www.lawguru.com.*

In Mississippi, it is illegal to teach

someone else about the concept of polygamy. *That's something we each must discover for ourselves.*

❯ "Mississippi," Dumblaws.com, *www.dumblaws.com.*

Before Jimmy Carter signed H.R. 1337 in 1978, it was illegal to brew your own beer at home. *The government should never limit the ways I can (and do) abuse my own body.*

❭ "History of Homebrewing," American Homebrewers Association, *www.home brewersassociation.org.*

Technically, Photoshopping a picture of a child's head onto the body of a pornographic film star could be considered child pornography in the United States. *The reverse isn't illegal, just creepy.*

❭ 18 U.S.C. § 2256. "Definitions for Chapter," Cornell University Law School, *www.law.cornell .edu.*

In Nevada, the lead vehicle of a funeral procession is permitted to run red lights. *The passenger is already dead anyway.*

❭ "Right-Of-Way of Funeral Processions," Connecticut General Assembly, March 12, 2004, *www.cga.ct.gov.*

New Jersey residents who have been convicted of driving while intoxicated are no longer eligible to apply for personalized license plates. *They can pry my Jovi4eva plate from my cold dead hands.*

❭ "New Jersey," Dumblaws. com, *www.dumblaws.com.*

> Ian Harrison, *Take Me to Your Leader* (Dorling Kindersley Ltd., 2007), 135.

Residents of Kentucky

must bathe at least once a year.
*They can make you bathe, but
they can't make you use soap.*

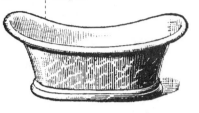

> Greg Williamson, "Jesus Arrested! San Francisco, April 17, 1879," Found San Francisco, *www.foundsf.org*.

While exiting the theater after his performance
in *The Passion* in 1879, actor James O'Neil was
arrested by San Francisco police for impersonat-
ing Jesus, a violation of city ordinances at the time.
Remember, it's not an impersonation if you believe it's real.

In Texas, it is illegal to shoot buffalo from the second floor of a hotel. *This is literally the only law in Texas.*

> "Stupid Laws In Texas," Stupidlaws.com, *www.stupidlaws.com.*

> Ian Lendler, *Alcoholica Esoterica: A Collection of Useful and Useless Information As It Relates to the History and Consumption of All Manner of Booze* (Penguin, 2005), 227.

**During prohibition, there were several
loopholes that allowed thirsty Americans** to
obtain alcohol legally. For example, doctors were
permitted to fill one hundred prescriptions for
medicinal whiskey every three months.
Finally, proof that booze is good for me.

After a thirteen-year-old boy was stabbed with a comb in Alabama, the state officially made it illegal to walk around with a comb concealed in one's pocket. *This is why we can't have nice things.*

❯ Ian Harrison, *Take Me to Your Leader* (Dorling Kindersley Ltd., 2007), 135.

As of 2011, there were nineteen states in the United States that allowed first cousins to marry. At the same time, only five states allowed members of the same sex to marry. *Yet my pet turtle and I must hide our love in shame. Disgusting.*

❯ "Cousin Marriage vs. Gay Marriage," *The Advocate*, June 1, 2011, *www.advocate.com*.

Treason is the only crime mentioned by name in the Constitution. *Treason is a horrible crime that should be punishable by death. Except for that one time against the British.*

❯ Erin Barrett and Jack Mingo, *Random Kinds Of Factness: 1001 (or So) Absolutely True Tidbits About (Mostly) Everything* (Conari Press, 2005), 6.

In the 1840s, lawmakers in Connecticut banned nine-pin bowling due to excessive gambling on the sport. To circumvent the law, players simply added a tenth pin, an element that is now a mainstay of the game. *Too bad that strategy rarely works: Possessing an ounce of pot is illegal you say? Well I've got ten ounces. Now what, suckers?*

> Arkady Leokum and K. R. Hobbie, *The Little Giant Book of Weird & Wacky Facts* (Sterling Publishing Company, 2005), 177.

The city of Urbana, Illinois, explicitly forbids monsters from entering the corporate limits.

Too late.

> Noel Botham, *The Mega Book of Useless Information* (John Blake, 2009), 246.

In 2011 San Francisco proposed legislation that would make it illegal to sit down on a public bench or other form of public seating while naked without first laying down a towel or other protective barrier. The only current restriction for nudity in the city is that the individual must not be aroused. *Unless it's a magic towel that lets me unsee the nudist, I don't see the point.*

> Rachel Gordon, "Dear Nudists: Please Cover Up, the Seat at Least," *San Francisco Chronicle*, September, 7, 2011, *www .sfgate.com.*

In Kentucky, you may not marry the same person more than three times. *Unless of course they promise they've really changed this time.*

> "53 Crazy Laws," Random History, *www.facts.random history.com.*

Fisherman in Wyoming are prohibited from using firearms as a means of catching fish. *Unless the fish are also armed, to give them a sporting chance.*

❯ "Stupid Laws In Wyoming," Stupidlaws.com, *www.stupid laws.com.*

Adults in Indiana may not consume beer in the presence of children.

Unless they are willing to share.

❯ Sheryl Lindsell-Roberts, K. R. Hobbie, Ted LeValliant, and Marcel Theroux, *Wacky Laws, Weird Decisions & Strange Statutes* (Main Street, 2004), 25.

In 1838 Missouri Governor Lilburn Boggs issued Executive Order 44, an edict that called for the immediate eviction of any and all Mormons in the state. The order was not officially rescinded until 1976. *"Unsolicited relocation" sounds way better than "eviction."*

❯ R. Scott Lloyd, "Former Missouri Governor Honored for Rescinding Mormon 'Extermination Order," *Deseret News,* May 31, 2010, *www.deseretnews.com.*

In 1919, Nebraska enacted a law that made it illegal to teach any subject in a language other than English. The law was deemed unconstitutional and repealed several years later. *We don't take kindly to foreigners in our country we in no way stole from the natives.*

❯ Austine Cline, "Decision: *Meyer v. Nebraska* (1923)," About.com, *www.about.com.*

Adultery is punishable with a $10 fine in Maryland. *Worth it.*

❯ Tim Murphy, "Map: Is Adultery Illegal," *Mother Jones*, November 29, 2011, *www.motherjones.com*.

In 2011, California Governor Jerry Brown passed a bill that made it mandatory for public schools to include the contributions of gay, lesbian, bisexual, and transgender individuals in their social studies curriculum. *Yet somehow the universe has yet to unravel.*

❯ Judy Lin, "California Gay History Law: Jerry Brown Signs Landmark Bill," *The Huffington Post*, July 14, 2011, *www.huffingtonpost.com*.

It is illegal to buy or sell a Medal of Honor. *Although you can still win it in that claw arcade game.*

❯ "Civil War Ames Sword & Scabbard," *Antiques Roadshow*, www.pbs.org.

First cousins may marry in Utah, but only if both parties are more than sixty-five years old. *They mean individually, not combined. Trust me, I tried.*

❯ "53 Crazy Laws," Random History, *www.facts.randomhistory.com*.

≈ CHAPTER 2 ≈

From Michael Jackson's Pet Chimp to New Mexico's Lesbian Lizards

Animal Oddities to Astound

Australia may have the grotesque lovechild of a duck and a beaver known as the platypus, but America is no slouch when it comes to strange wildlife. If you want to see a mole with a starfish where its face should be, or a worm that literally melts when you remove it from its icy home, you need look no further than next door.

Over the course of thirty years, Professor Con Slobodchikoff of Northern Arizona University discovered that prairie dogs have developed an intricate language to warn one another against predators. Through various calls, they can differentiate between a coyote and a domestic dog as well as describe individual humans based on the color of their clothing. *"Hey guys, here comes the sad human with the red tape recorder and no friends again."*

❭ Jad Abumrad and Robert Krulwich, "New Language Discovered: Prairiedogese," NPR, January 20, 2011, *www.npr.org.*

❭ Glen Vecchione, *A Little Giant Book: Science Facts* (Sterling Publishing, 2007), 101.

Gallstones extracted from animals were commonly used to treat wounds in nineteenth-century America. Doctors believed chemicals in the stones prevented infection. *Actually, I'm pretty sure they caused them.*

❭ "Mating Behavior of Banana Slugs," Neatorama, July 26, 2007, *www.neatorama.com.*

Like most slugs, the North American banana slug is a hermaphrodite. Unlike most slugs, after two individuals mate, it is not uncommon for one individual to bite off the penis of the other in a process called apophallation. *And now you can't unknow that.*

❭ "Monsters Inside Me: The Brain-Eating Amoeba," Animal Planet, *www.animal.discovery .com.*

Dubbed "the brain-eating amoeba," *Naegleria fowleri* is a parasite found in 70 percent of U.S. lakes. It hijacks the victim's brain and causes confusion, hallucinations, and loss of motor function. Death can occur in as few as seven days. *All the more reason to spend your summers underground in an air–filtered bunker, huddled in the fetal position.*

Since 1955, park officials at Disneyland have maintained feeding stations to accommodate an army of feral cats that prowl the grounds at night to keep the park free of rodents. *Also to put down an insurrection should Mickey get uppity.*

> Adam K. Raymond, *www .mentalfloss.com,* "8 secrets about Disneyland," CNN Living, July 1, 2011, *www.cnn.com.*

Each fall, millions of monarch butterflies leave the United States and migrate south to Mexico. Some butterflies travel as many as 3,000 miles to reach their destination. *They are the elderly grandparents of the insect world.*

> "Monarch Butterfly," *National Geographic, www.animals .nationalgeographic.com.*

A group of ferrets is called a "business." *But they prefer the term "job creators."*

> "Interesting Questions, Facts, and Information," Funtrivia, *www.funtrivia.com.*

In order to develop a universal pain scale for insect stings, American researcher Justin Schmidt and his team sacrificed their own bodies in the name of science. Over the course of their study, they subjected themselves to numerous stings from seventy-eight different species of insect. *A.K.A. what insect scientists do when they're drunk and bored.*

> Debbie Hadley, "Schmidt Pain Index of Insect Stings," About .com, *www.about.com.*

Polar bear milk is 35 percent fat.

And very difficult to harvest.

> "Polar Bear," San Diego Zoo. *www.sandiegozoo.org.*

The largest swarm of insects ever recorded consisted of approximately 12.5 trillion Rocky Mountain locusts that flew over Nebraska for ten days in 1874. *Which is why I carry a cyanide capsule at all times.*

> Lisa Levitt Ryckman, "The Great Locust Mystery," *Rocky Mountain News, www.denver .rockymountainnews.com/ millenium/0622mile.shtml.*

Although monarch butterflies migrate both north and south, the same butterfly never makes both trips. The monarchs die shortly after they reach their destination, but not before laying their eggs. It is their descendants that later make the return trip, with the route somehow programmed into their DNA. *A genetic gift infinitely more useful than hitchhiker's thumb.*

> "Monarch Butterfly," *National Geographic, www.animals .nationalgeographic.com.*

The ruby-throated hummingbird beats its wings up to fifty-three times per second. *And yes, there is one trapped in your cell phone. You monster.*

> "Ruby-Throated Humming-bird," *National Geographic, www.animals.national geographic.com.*

One cat or dog is euthanized every eight seconds in an American shelter. *You're a horrible person if you change the channel the moment you hear Sarah McLachlan's voice.*

> "Pet Overpopulation," Humane Society, *www.humanesociety.com.*

Supai, Arizona, and the nearby Phantom Ranch village are the only two places in the country that have their mail delivered by mule. *At least the mule doesn't judge you by your magazine subscriptions.*

> "Special Delivery: Mail By Mule," CBS News, November 10, 2009, *www.cbsnews.com.*

The Eastern spotted skunk

does a handstand before it sprays. *And so do I.*

> *National Geographic Kids, Weird But True: 300 Outrageous Facts* (*National Geographic* Children's Books, 2009), 34.

At thirty-seven inches, the longest tapeworm ever extracted from a human belonged to Sally Mae Wallace of Great Grits, Minnesota. *Congratulations?*

> "15 World Records of Shame," Herald Daily, January 11, 2010, *www.heralddaily.com.*

An alligator can survive up to three years without eating.

Best. Pet. Ever.

> Marshall Brain, "How Alligators Work," How Stuff Works, *www.science.howstuffworks.com*.

Biologists at the University of Wyoming have bred genetically altered silkworms that can spin the same super-strong silk spiders use to construct their webs. They hope to use the harvested silk to engineer everything from artificial ligaments to body armor. *Can your God do that?*

> Rebecca Boyle, "How Modified Worms and Goats Can Mass-Produce Nature's Toughest Fiber," *Popular Science*, October 6, 2010, *www.popsci.com*.

A male woodchuck is called a **"he-chuck."** *Biologists are nothing if not unimaginative.*

> *National Geographic Kids, Weird but True! 3: 300 Outrageous Facts* (*National Geographic* Children's Books, 2011), 68.

California condors can fly to heights of 15,000 feet and often travel as far as 150 miles in search of food. *Clever defense mechanism. Rednecks don't shoot at things that high up. Mostly.*

❯ "California Condor," Defenders of Wildlife, *www.defenders.org.*

The longest recorded swim for a polar bear was 426 miles over the course of nine straight days. *Brace yourselves, they're coming south.*

❯ Anne Casselman, "Longest Polar Bear Swim Recorded—426 Miles Straight," *National Geographic, www.news.nationalgeographic.com.*

In 2009, high tech giant Google revealed a very low-tech solution to dealing with overgrown fields at the company's Mountain View headquarters. They rented a team of 200 goats to chomp on the grass and trim it down to size. *Damn goats. Always taking jobs away from honest, hard-working Americans.*

❯ "Mowing with Goats," Google Blog, May 1, 2009, *www.googleblog.blogspot.com.*

Despite its ubiquity, the Rocky Mountain locust was driven to extinction in just twenty years thanks to a nationwide effort to eradicate the insect. Americans used everything from oil and water to dynamite to kill the pests. *Your move, God.*

❯ Lisa Levitt Ryckman, "The Great Locust Mystery," *Rocky Mountain News,* http://denver .rockymountainnews.com/ millennium/0622mile.shtml.

In 2003, a truck carrying a shipment of bees
overturned while traveling on I-95 in Florida, killing the driver and releasing all 80 million specimens into the wild. The resulting swarm stopped traffic for hours. *Death by steering wheel is always better than death by 80 million bee stings.*

❯ "80 Million Bees Released In Fatal I-95 Crash," Click Orlando, April 7, 2003, *www.clickorlando.com.*

Domestic pigs may be much smarter than we originally thought.
Not only can they recognize themselves in a mirror (an ability we once believed was specific to humans and great apes), but they can also be trained to make wordlike sounds on command, herd sheep, close and open cages, and even play videogames with joysticks. *Give him a beard and some Mountain Dew and you've got yourself a new best friend.*

❯ Natalie Angier, "Pigs Prove to Be Smart, if Not Vain," *The New York Times*, November 9, 2009, *www.nytimes.com.*

Because former Detroit Lions runningback
Barry Sanders was such an unpredictable player, the defensive coach of the Minnesota Vikings had his defensive linemen chase chickens around in practice before facing the Lions. *He also just wanted to see if they'd do it.*

❯ Torrey Laffoon, "A Tribute To Barry Sanders: What Made Him Great," Bleacher Report, December 2, 2009, *www.bleacherreport.com.*

According to the game's manual, Mario
was the real villain in the original Donkey Kong game. He abused his giant ape pet, which eventually got sick of his mistreatment and escaped. *He was just misunderstood. Like that dog in* Cujo.

❯ Steve Blair, "5 Classic Games You Didn't Know Had WTF Backstories," July 24, 2011, *Cracked*, *www.cracked.com.*

When a circus elephant named Mary attacked and killed one of her trainers in 1916, Tennessee officials insisted circus owner Charlie Sparks dispose of the dangerous animal. The following day, Sparks attached a chain to her neck and hoisted her up on a railroad derrick until she died. She remains the first and only elephant to be killed by hanging in the United States. *I don't want to live on this planet anymore.*

❯ Stephanie Dixon, "The Hanging of Mary the Elephant," *Tennessee Journalist*, September 13, 2009, *www.tnjn.com.*

The Muir Glacier in Alaska is home to the ice worm, a curious creature just a few centimeters long that tunnels through the ice in search of food. It is very sensitive to heat, and can liquefy if exposed to temperatures above 40°F. *I have an idea. Grab a magnifying glass and meet me in Alaska.*

❯ Sandi Doughton, "Ice Worms: They're Real, and They're Hot," *The Seattle Times*, February 21, 2006, *www.seattletimes.com.*

Garfield's favorite movie is *Old Yeller*, due mostly to the film's "happy ending." *I see what he did there.*

❯ Dane Sherwood, Sandy Wood, and Kara Kovalchik, *The Pocket Idiot's Guide to Not So Useless Facts* (Penguin Group, 2006), 45.

The United States is the only country other than Gabon that allows the use of chimpanzees for human disease testing. *I vote we use seagulls instead. Annoying bastards.*

❯ "Ban Chimp Testing," *Scientific American*, October, 2011, *www.scientificamerican.com.*

Almost two-thirds of U.S. dog owners

sign their pet's name to letters and cards. *If you do this, your dog secretly prays for your death.*

❯ Noel Botham, *The Mega Book of Useless Information* (John Blake, 2009), 333.

The greater siren is a primitive salamander native to the East Coast that lacks hind limbs and is completely aquatic. If its watery home dries up, it burrows into the mud and encases itself in a cocoon of mucus to aestivate. It can survive up to a year in this dormant state, where its body functions slow by as much as 70 percent. *I would only use this power if I could fit an Xbox and a quesadilla maker into my fortress of snot.*

❯ "Greater Siren," Smithsonian National Zoological Park, *www.nationalzoo.si.edu.*

The only bird known to hibernate is the North American whippoorwill. While it rests, its internal temperature plummets more than 55°F. *It's actually just a really small, flying bear.*

❯ Russell Ash, *Firefly's World of Facts* (Firefly Books, 2007), 58.

Native to marshlands in the northeastern United States and parts of Canada, the star-nosed mole is so named because it possesses eleven pairs of fleshy growths circling its snout. The strange appendage contains more than 25,000 minute sensory receptors and helps the creature feel its way around its dark, damp world. *I've seen uglier things in my day. But not many.*

❯ Kenneth C. Catania, "A Star Is Born," *Natural History*, June 2000, *www.naturalhistorymag.com.*

In the 1970s, stories of a half man, half chimp "humanzee" named Oliver took the nation by storm. Unlike an ordinary chimp, Oliver walked upright and also possessed a smaller, less hairy skull and nose. Although several scientists who examined Oliver confirmed he was nothing more than an ordinary chimpanzee with human-like features, they could not account for his taste for expensive sherry and cigars. *I've seen* Planet of the Apes. *This will only end in tears.*

❯ Jordan Smith, "Famous Long Ago," *The Austin Chronicle*, December 15, 2006, *www.austinchronicle.com.*

The North American pronghorn may only be the second fastest land mammal, but unlike the cheetah —which gets winded after about a quarter mile—it can sustain its impressive fifty-three-mile-per-hour sprint for several miles at a time. *If it came to a fight, though, my money's still on the animal with canines.*

❯ "Pronghorn," *National Geographic, www.animals .nationalgeographic.com.*

Because of the 1.5 million traffic accidents they cause each year, **white-tailed deer are technically the most dangerous mammals** in America. *If you think deer are cute, you've obviously never picked one out of your grill.*

❯ Ronald Bailey, "North America's Most Dangerous Mammal," *Reason* magazine, November 21, 2001, *www.reason.com.*

The reason most firehouses have spiral staircases is because before the invention of the automobile, fire trucks were pulled by horses. The circular stairs prevented the horses from climbing the stairs and injuring themselves if they happened to break out of the stables. *It also protects from zombie attacks. Probably.*

❯ Glen Vecchione, Joel Harris, Sharon Harris, *A Little Giant Book: Science Facts* (Sterling, 2007), 14.

Relative to its size, the barnacle

has the largest penis of any other animal. *Maybe for now. But I saw an ad on this website . . .*

❯ "The Discovernator," Discovery Channel, *www.news.discovery.com*.

The unicorn-like tusk of the narwhal, a whale species occasionally spotted off the coast of Alaska, is actually an enlarged tooth that grows from the upper jaw of the animal. No one is certain what function the tusk serves, but scientists speculate it might be a secondary sexual characteristic, similar to a lion's mane. *It's also great for spearing bacon.*

❯ "Narwhal," Defenders of Wildlife, *www.defenders.org*.

Native to the southwestern United States, the gila monster is one of only two species of venomous lizards. Unlike a snake, which injects its venom through hollow fangs, the gila monster bites its victim and then locks its jaw so it can chew the toxin into its prey. *It's nice when animals are aptly named.*

❯ "Gila Monster," Smithsonian National Zoological Park, *www.nationalzoo.si.edu*.

The North American kangaroo rat can go its entire life without ever taking a sip of water. It can survive from the moisture contained within various seeds. *Must be nice to be so awesome.*

> ❯ Animal Fact Sheet: Merriam's Kangaroo Rat, Arizona-Sonora Desert Museum, *www.desert museum.org.*

On July 2, 2005, Kenneth Pinyan of Seattle, Washington, died while participating in anal intercourse with a male horse. A documentary of the encounter called *Zoo* was one of sixteen winners at the 2007 Sundance Film Festival. *Never underestimate the allure of bestiality.*

> ❯ Top 25 Craziest Deaths," 2Spare.com, March 23, 2006, *www.2spare.com.*

If a deer becomes dehydrated, its urine can turn blue. *Not a very good survival technique.*

> ❯ Noel Botham, *The Mega Book of Useless Information* (John Blake, 2009), 54.

In early 2011, Sal Esposito of Boston, Massachusetts, was summoned for jury duty, despite the fact that he was actually a domestic shorthaired cat. The Boston census allows residents to list their pets, which caused the error. His owners filed for his disqualification on the basis that he "was unable to speak and understand English." *No matter how much you think your cat loves you, he'd put you away for life without a second thought.*

> ❯ Lorianna De Giorgio, "Boston Cat Called for Jury Duty," *Toronto Star*, January 14, 2011, *www.thestar.com.*

The burrowing owl of North America is so named because, unlike most species of owl, it nests and roosts underground. Although they prefer to steal holes dug by small mammals like prairie dogs, they can excavate their own if necessary. *Nothing could be more American than walking into somebody's home and exclaiming, "I live here now!"*

❯ "Burrowing Owl," Defenders of Wildlife, *www.defenders.org*.

Pigeons never forget a face. If you chase one away, it will avoid you should you encounter it again. *I wonder if they can remember the bottom of my shoe.*

❯ "Pigeons Never Forget a Face," *ScienceDaily*, July 3, 2011, *www.sciencedaily.com*.

New York City is home to an estimated 1,000,0000 pigeons.
I'll get my slingshot.

❯ Courtney Gross, "Problems with Pigeons," *Gotham Gazette*, November 26, 2007, *www.gothamgazette.com*.

The North American turkey was named for what was mistakenly assumed to be its country of origin. *Our ancestors were no better at geography than we are.*

❯ Glen Vecchione, Joel Harris, Sharon Harris, *A Little Giant Book: Science Facts* (Sterling, 2007), 17.

Kentucky produces 95 percent of the world's bourbon. At any given time, the state is home to more than 5 million barrels of aging whiskey. *Our mission is clear. We must invade and pillage Kentucky.*

❯ Associated Press, "KY Distilleries Rapidly Expand Amid Bourbon Boom," Yahoo! News, July 21, 2011, *www.news.yahoo.com.*

One of the most popular cure-alls in nineteenth-century America was a concoction called "snail water." The remedy was made by pounding snails and earthworms into a paste and then boiling the mixture in ale with herbs. It was then bottled and drunk as a tonic. *Remember this fact if you ever long to travel back in time.*

❯ George W. Givens, *500 Little-Known Facts in U.S. History* (Cedar Fort, 2006), 148.

If you ever come across an odoriferous, waxy substance when walking on one of America's many beaches, it might behoove you to take it home. It could be valuable ambergris, a substance secreted in the stomach of sperm whales and a crucial ingredient in some of the world's most expensive perfumes. *Sadly, most perfumists can tell the difference between ambergris and worthless human vomit. Trust me.*

❯ Corey Kilgannon, "Please Let It Be Whale Vomit, Not Just Sea Junk," *The New York Times*, December 18, 2006, *www.nytimes.com.*

Due to chemicals it absorbs from the toxic newts upon which it preys, the Oregon garter snake is one of only two truly "poisonous" snakes in the world. Many species that are mistakenly referred to as "poisonous" are actually "venomous." *Semantics can be deadly.*

❯ "Snakes" Aquatic Community, *www.aquaticcommunity.com.*

The average pigeon

produces twenty-five pounds of waste each year. *So do the world a favor: Kill a pigeon.*

❯ Sheila McClear, "The New Pigeon Wars," *New York Post*, February 21, 2010, *www.nypost.com*.

On display at the Smithsonian Institution stands Cher Ami ("Dear Friend"), a stuffed carrier pigeon that served during World War I. After being shot and suffering a shattered leg and broken breastbone, Cher struggled back into the air and flew twenty-five miles to deliver a message that saved the lives of nearly 200 American soldiers. He received a special medal for gallantry for his service, and is the highest decorated fowl in American history. *So, naturally, we stuffed him and put him on display. The highest honor the military can bestow.*

❯ George W. Givens, *500 Little-Known Facts in U.S. History* (Cedar Fort, 2006), 245.

A shrew must eat more than three times its own body weight each day to avoid starvation. *So best to eat them at the end of the day, for optimal nutritional benefit.*

❯ "The Discovernator," Discovery Channel, *www.news.discovery.com*.

Every year, the bar-tailed godwit bird flies from Alaska to New Zealand—without stopping. The 6,835-mile journey takes the bird approximately eight days. *So no, the gym is not "too far" to walk to.*

❯ "Bar-Tailed Godwit Sets Record for Long-Distance Flight," *ScienceDaily*, June 9, 2010, *www.sciencedaily.com*.

A skunk's skin is striped

underneath its fur. *Sucks to be the guy who had to confirm that.*

> *National Geographic Kids, Weird but True! 3: 300 Outrageous Facts (National Geographic Children's Books, 2011), 56.*

Bull sharks are one of only two shark species capable of surviving in fresh water. A specimen was once caught more than 1,700 miles up the Mississippi River. *So the terrified feeling you get when your foot touches lake weeds is justified.*

> Brian Handwerk, "Shark Facts: Attack Stats, Record Swims, More," *National Geographic,* June 13, 2005, *www.news .nationalgeographic.com.*

Earthworms are not native to the United States, and are actually an invasive species introduced by early European settlers. *Thanks, assholes.*

> "The Discovernator," Discovery Channel, *www.news.discovery.com.*

During much of his career, Michael Jackson traveled with a pet chimp he affectionately named "Bubbles." The two were so close that Bubbles slept in a crib next to Jackson's bed and ate at the dinner table. In 2005, Jackson revealed that the two even shared a toilet. *That's disgusting. No self-respecting chimp would ever share a bathroom with Michael Jackson.*

❯ "Monkey Business in the Loo," *The Sydney Morning Herald*, May 12, 2005, *www.smh .com.au.*

Chuck Wepner, the real-life inspiration for the *Rocky* films, fought a full-grown Kodiak bear on two separate occasions during his career. *The bear didn't so much "fight him" as "choose not to kill him."*

❯ "ESPN to Televise Film about 'The Real Rocky,'" ESPN, *www.espn.go.com.*

The bowhead whale, which is often spotted off the coast of Alaska, is one of the longest-living animals on earth. Scientists have confirmed that at least some specimens have lived as long as 150 to 200 years. *That's just because they aren't delicious enough for us to hunt.*

❯ John Roach, "Rare Whales Can Live to Nearly 200, Eye Tissue Reveals," *National Geographic*, July 13, 2006, *www .news.nationalgeographic.com.*

Despite popular belief, cows do not sleep standing up. They are also quite capable of righting themselves if tipped over on their side. *The secret to successful cow tipping is finding something better to do.*

❯ Ian Denomme, "Cow-Tipping a Moo-yth?" *The Gazette*, November 9, 2005, *www.gazette.uwo.ca/article.cfm?section=Fro ntPage&articleID=465&month=11&day=9&year=2005.*

Many shelters across the country ban the adoption of black cats in the weeks leading up to Halloween, for fear they might be used for ritual sacrifices. *There's other uses for them?*

> Rebecca Wallwork, "Black Cats: Cute or Cursed?" *New York Post*, November 7, 2010, *www.nypost.com.*

The U.S. Navy keeps a team of sea lions in California that have been trained to identify active mines and even to subdue enemy divers. *They may look silly on land, but step into the water and you are their bitch.*

> Lizzie Smith, "Forget the Seals, Meet the Navy Sea Lions," *Daily Mail*, November 26, 2009, *www.dailymail.co.uk.*

At more than 4,800 years old, a Great Basin bristlecone pine tree located in California's White Mountains is the oldest living organism on earth. Scientists named it the Methuselah Tree after the biblical character who lived to the age of 969. *Just imagine all the stupid crap that tree has seen humans do.*

> Don Bain, "Methuselah Tree," PBS, *www.pbs.org.*

The California government refuses to release the exact location of the Methuselah Tree in order to protect it from vandalism. *I don't want to hurt it. I only want to steal the secret of its power.*

> Don Bain, "Methuselah Tree," PBS, *www.pbs.org.*

Eastern diamondback rattlesnakes can give birth up to five years after mating. *Which is one good reason not to have sex with rattlesnakes. But certainly not the only reason.*

❯ "The Discovernator," Discovery Channel, *www.news.discovery.com.*

To win a bull-riding contest, a rodeo cowboy need only stay on the bull for eight seconds. Few ever make it. *Trust me, even if they win, it's so mindless we all lose.*

❯ Noel Botham, *The Bumper Book of Useless Information: An Official Useless Information Society Publication* (John Blake, 2008), 330.

Squirrels are immune to rabies.

Unfortunately, they are not immune to rocks.

❯ Dane Sherwood, Sandy Wood, and Kara Kovalchik, *The Pocket Idiot's Guide to Not So Useless Facts* (Penguin Group, 2006).

Biologists have identified several species of lizard in America's desert regions that are able to procreate without the presence of males. The females bypass typical reproduction practices and instead lay unfertilized eggs that grow into genetic copies of the mother. *Well, men, the end is near. We had a good run.*

❯ "Sexes: Leapin' Lizards!" *Time,* February 18, 1980, *www.time.com.*

Edgewater, New Jersey, is home to a small colony of about 200 monk parakeets, a species indigenous to South America. The population has lived in the town since the 1960s, although nobody is quite certain how they got there. *Well, pet parakeets are notoriously difficult to flush. You do the math.*

❯ David Holmberg, "Defending the Parrots of Edgewater," December 7, 2008, *The New York Times*, www.nytimes.com.

During World War II, the United States government briefly considered using domesticated pigeons to guide bombs toward enemies. Dubbed "Project Pigeon," the program was scrapped when more reliable guidance systems became available. *What could be more reliable than a creature with the brain the size of a peanut?*

❯ Julie S. Vargas, *A Brief Biography of B. F. Skinner* (B. F. Skinner Foundation, 2005), *www.bfskinner.org*.

The female sand tiger shark produces multiple eggs, but typically only one pup emerges from each of her two uteri. This is because the first embryos to develop teeth will instinctively cannibalize the rest. *When it comes to sibling rivalry, a pre-emptive strike is almost always the answer.*

❯ Molly Edmonds, "How Are Shark Pups Born?" How Stuff Works, *www.science.howstuffworks.com*.

The brain of a cockroach resides inside its body instead of its head. As a result, it can survive for up to nine days if decapitated. *This goes against everything I know about zombies.*

❯ "The Discovernator," Discovery Channel, *www.newsdiscovery.com*.

The venom of the black widow spider is fifteen times more deadly than that of a rattlesnake. *Which is why my house is patrolled by a team of fifteen rattlesnakes. And subsequently why I don't live there.*

❯ "Black Widow Spider," *National Geographic, www.animals.national geographic.com.*

Despite a lack of education or formal training working with grizzly bears, former drug addict and wildlife enthusiast Timothy Treadwell spent thirteen consecutive summers in Alaska documenting his encounters with some of America's largest predators. Videos of his encounters show many of the bears tolerating his presence, with some even allowing him close enough to touch them. His complete trust of the animals proved his undoing, as he and his girlfriend were attacked and killed by a rogue bear in 2003.
Apparently bears don't like it when you pet them.

❯ Carig Medred, "Wildlife Author Killed, Eaten By Bears He Loved," *Anchorage Daily News*, October 9, 2003, *www.adn.com.*

Despite his insistence that his presence in no way provoked the bears in Katmai National Park, Treadwell's death was the first since the park's establishment in 1918. *Treadwell never fathered any children. Way to go, Darwinism.*

❯ Kevin Sanders, "Night of the Grizzly," Yellowstone Bearman, *www.yellowstone-bearman.com.*

In 1990, a lone flamingo named Pink Floyd escaped from Salt Lake City's Tracy Aviary and settled on the shores of the Great Salt Lake where he lived alone for at least fourteen years. In 2004, fans of the bird erected ten life-size plastic flamingos along the beach to keep him company.
You know what's more depressing than an army of plastic friends? Yeah, me neither.

❯ Leigh Dethman, "Pink Floyd Gets Stoic Pals," *Deseret News*, March 11, 2004, *www.deseret news.com*.

Despite popular belief, the nine-banded armadillo cannot roll itself into a ball to escape predators. It possesses too many bony plates. *I don't know what to believe anymore.*

❯ "A Quick List of Armadillo Quirks!," Michigan State University, *www.msu.edu*.

Armadillos can pass leprosy to humans. *So cute, so terrifying.*

❯ Richard W. Truman, Ph.D., Pushpendra Singh, Ph.D., Rahul Sharma, Ph.D., Philippe Busso, Jacques Rougemont, Ph.D., Alberto Paniz-Mondolfi, M.D., Adamandia Kapopoulou, M.S., Sylvain Brisse, Ph.D., David M. Scollard, M.D., Ph.D., Thomas P. Gillis, Ph.D., and Stewart T. Cole, Ph.D., "Probable Zoonotic Leprosy in the Southern United States," *The New England Journal of Medicine*, April 28, 2011, *www.nejm.org*.

The nine-banded armadillo is the only mammal that always gives birth to four identical offspring. They each form from the same egg and even share one placenta. *When it comes to children, it's always good to have spares. Just in case . . .*

❯ "A Quick List of Armadillo Quirks!," Michigan State University, *www.msu.edu*.

A female codfish may lay as many as 5,000,000 eggs simultaneously. *Your monthly visitor doesn't sound so bad now, does it, ladies?*

❯Dane Sherwood, Sandy Wood, and Kara Kovalchik, *The Pocket Idiot's Guide to Not So Useless Facts* (Penguin Group, 2006).

In 2007, ecologists discovered a beaver dam so large it could be seen from space. The dam spans a staggering 2,800 feet and has likely been under construction since the 1970s. *Sort of puts that crappy set of shelves you built last year into perspective.*

❯ Michel Comte and Jacques Lemieux, "Largest Beaver Dam Seen From Space," Discovery News, May 6, 2010, *www.news.discovery.com.*

A beaver can hold its breath for forty-five minutes. *Smug little bastards.*

❯ "The Discovernator," Discovery Channel, *www.news.discovery.com.*

Scientists once thought the blue whale to be the largest living organism, but the honor actually belongs to a fungus in Oregon. An individual specimen of *armillaria ostoyae* fungus spans 2,384 acres of the state's Blue Mountain region. *We should probably "take care" of that soon, before it becomes self aware.*

❯ Anne Casselman, "Strange but True: The Largest Organism on Earth Is a Fungus," *Scientific American*, October 4, 2007, *www.scientificamerican.com.*

✦ CHAPTER 3 ✦

Aliens, Jackalopes, Wandering Stones, Gravity Hills, and More

The Wonderful World of the American Paranormal to Terrify

The United States is by no means the only country with paranormal activity, but it is definitely home to the strangest. The world's first reported alien abduction? Check. A swirling vortex that makes you taller? Double check. A giant spaghetti monster that created the universe and plagues humanity with natural disasters due to a general decline in the pirate population? Huh?

It's easy to dismiss the facts in this chapter as fantasy, but before you do, consider this: Can you prove that Lake Champlain *isn't* inhabited by a man-eating dinosaur?

Since the first UFO sightings, more than 20 million Americans have come forward claiming to have seen UFOs. *<sarcasm>How can 20 million people be wrong? </sarcasm>*

❯ Gary Bates, *Alien Intrusion* (Creation Book Publishers, 2010), 16.

On October 21, 1967, members of the folk band the Fugs attempted to exorcise the Pentagon. The process culminated with members of the band invoking the help of several ancient gods and goddesses to levitate the structure—a feat that was unsuccessful. *Actually, the building burrowed into the ground and turned into a giant mole crab. But only if you were on acid.*

❯ History, The Fugs, *www.thefugs.com.*

United States patent number 4,429,685 is a surgical procedure for creating unicorns. The process involves transplanting the horn buds of newly born cows, antelope, sheep, or goats to a central position on the front of the animal's skull. *And then?*

❯ Ian Harrison, *Take Me to Your Leader* (Dorling Kindersley Ltd., 2007), 123.

While shooting the 2005 film *Batman Begins* in Chicago, a driver accidentally crashed into the Batmobile. He was apparently drunk, and panicked when he believed the vehicle to be an invading alien spacecraft. *Because when I see a spaceship, my gut instinct is to kamikaze into it.*

❯ "Batman Begins Trivia," IMDb, *www.imdb.com.*

Tired of waiting for the messiah to appear, in 1853 John Murray Spear and his followers decided to construct their own. The group gathered at a hilltop in Lynn, Massachusetts, to build "the New Motive Power," a robot messiah constructed of copper, steel, and a host of magnets. Unfortunately for Spear and his followers, their creation failed to ever spring to life. *Be patient. We'll be ruled by robots soon enough.*

> Robert Damon Schneck, "John Murray Spear's God Machine," *Fortean Times*, May 2002, *www.forteantimes.com.*

Due to the negative connotations associated with the number thirteen, the thirteenth day of each month costs the United States an estimated $83 million in absenteeism from work and train and plane cancellations. *Better safe and stupid than dead and sorry.*

> Russell Ash, *Firefly's World of Facts* (Firefly Books, 2007), 173.

The medical billing code for an **injury sustained as the result of a spaceship** is E845.0.

"Sir, we can't remove the alien larvae until we figure out how to bill your insurance provider."

> "2009 ICD-9-CM Diagnosis Code E845.0," ICD9 Data, *www.icd9data.com.*

Nearly one-third of the 6 million Americans who tuned in to Orson Welles's famous broadcast of *War of the Worlds* in 1938 believed the Earth was actually under alien attack. *Better to err on the side of caution when it comes to alien invaders.*

❯ Richard J. Hand, *Terror on the Air!: Horror Radio in America, 1931–1952* (McFarland & Company, 2006), 7.

Rather than shy away from their celestial town name, residents of Mars, Pennsylvania, decided to embrace it by erecting a spaceship statue in one of the town's parks with the plaque that reads: "May peace prevail on Earth." *Clever aliens. Hiding in plain sight.*

❯ Val Bromann, "15 of the Weirdest Roadside Attractions in America," *BootsnAll*, May 24, 2011, *www.bootsnall.com*.

In 2010, an animal control officer near Fort Worth, Texas, killed a strange-looking creature that residents claimed was actually the first captured specimen of the blood-sucking chupacabra monster. DNA tests later revealed the animal to be a coyote-canine hybrid with a bad case of skin mites. *Close enough.*

❯ Lita Beck, "Ugly? Yes. But El Chupacabra? Not So Much," NBCDFW, July 14, 2010, *www .nbcdfw.com*.

In 1971, Gerald Mayo brought a case to the western district court of Pennsylvania against Satan, claiming the defendant had caused his downfall and violated his constitutional rights. The judge threw the case out when Mayo failed to produce a home address for the Prince of Darkness. *Considering who was in office at the time, 1600 Pennsylvania Avenue would have been a safe bet.*

❯ Jason Zasky, "Devil's Advocate," *Failure Magazine*, *www .failuremag.com*.

One of the first known photographs of a UFO was that of a rocket-shaped object taken by a New Hampshire resident in 1870—more than thirty years before the Wright Brothers made their first flight. *Could have been time-traveling humans posing as aliens.*

❯ Joshua Gee, *Encyclopedia Horrifica* (Scholastic, 2007), 20.

On September 19, 1961, Betty and Barney Hill became the first Americans to claim to be abducted by aliens. While driving on a New Hampshire highway, the couple alleged a strange aircraft chased them for several minutes before they blacked out and came to two hours later and thirty-five miles ahead in their journey. After the incident, the couple discovered their watches had stopped working and there were now shiny circles on the trunk of their car that caused the needle of a compass to spin rapidly. *Did they have crystal meth in the sixties? If so, I may have a theory . . .*

❯ Lee Speigel, "Betty And Barney Hill UFO Abduction Story Commemorated On Official N.H. Highway Plaque," *The Huffington Post*, July 25, 2011, *www.huffingtonpost.com.*

While most people are aware of the first three kinds of close encounters with extra terrestrials (sighting of a UFO; observation of the physical effects produced by a UFO; contact), there are actually seven classifications, with the final being an instance where aliens mate with humans to create an alien/human hybrid. *Doesn't matter, had sex.*

❯ Joshua Gee, *Encyclopedia Horrifica* (Scholastic, 2007), 20.

In April 1995, *Discover magazine* published an article claiming that a new species of hairless, pink, mole-like creatures dubbed "hotheaded naked ice borers" were preying upon innocent penguins. Thankfully the story turned out to be an April Fools' Day hoax. *Exactly. Everyone knows hotheaded naked ice borers are afraid of penguins.*

> Joshua Gee, *Encyclopedia Horrifica* (Scholastic, 2007), 116.

In the event it should encounter alien life, the *Voyager* spacecraft launched in 1977 contained 12-inch gold-plated copper disks encoded with sounds that portray the diversity of life and culture on Earth—such as crickets chirping, bird songs, and greetings in fifty-five languages, as well as a recording of Chuck Berry performing "Johnny B. Goode." The disks also contain symbolic instructions on how to play them. *Future Headline: "Hipster Aliens Visit Earth; Liked It Better On Vinyl."*

> "What is the Golden Record," NASA, *www.nasa.gov.*

Several months after overzealous fan Steve Bartman interfered with a foul ball and cost the Chicago Cubs the 2003 National League Championship, a local restaurateur decided the cursed ball had to be destroyed. He purchased it for $113,824 and detonated it with the help of a Hollywood special effects team. *I've read enough fantasy novels to know you can't destroy cursed objects that easily.*

> Associated Press, "Cubs' Truly 'Foul' Ball Blown Up," NBC Sports, February 27, 2004, *www.nbcsports.msnbc.com.*

Shortly after its destruction, the remains of the Bartman Ball were boiled, and the captured steam was used to make a special pasta sauce. *Thus spreading the curse to legions of hungry customers.*

> Associated Press, "Cubs' Truly 'Foul' Ball Blown Up," NBC Sports, February 27, 2004, *www.nbcsports.msnbc.com.*

Lake Wales, Florida, is home to Spook Hill, a street where everything from cars to tennis balls and even water run uphill. Some believe the hill to be haunted, but scientists insist it is merely an optical illusion. *Ghosts have better things to do than push balls up hills. Like possess toasters and mess with ham radio enthusiasts.*

> Phyllis Goldman, *Monkeyshines on Strange and Wonderful Facts* (Monkeyshines, 1991), 10.

During the filming of The *Passion of the Christ*, the actor who played Jesus, Jim Caviezel, was struck by lightning while filming the Sermon on the Mount. *God might not have objected to the film, but Mother Nature sure as hell did.*

> "The Passion of the Christ," IMDb, *www.imdb.com.*

Only 7 percent of Americans
don't believe in some form of the paranormal (UFOs, ghosts, etc.). *I weep for the future.*

> Marley Gibson, Patrick Burns, and Dave Schrader, *The Other Side: A Teen's Guide to Ghost Hunting and the Paranormal* (Graphia, 2009), xi.

Unidentifiable masses of biological material that routinely wash up on coasts are known as "globsters." Although usually chunks of whale meat, numerous specimens—like one that washed ashore in St. Augustine, Florida, in 1896—have never been identified. *Grandma?*

❯ John Moore, "The St. Augustine Giant Octopus," *Strange Magazine, www.strangemag.com.*

More than half of all Americans

believe that guardian angels have aided them at some point in their lives. *I'd make a snarky comment about angels, but then they might stop helping me.*

❯ David Van Biema, "Guardian Angels Are Here, Say Most Americans," *Time,* September 18, 2008, *www.time.com.*

Conspiracy theorists insist that in 1943 the U.S. government conducted an experiment in Philadelphia to turn the USS *Eldridge* invisible. Instead, the ship allegedly teleported some 300 miles south to Norfolk, Virginia, and lost several crew members in the process, while the bodies of others were fused to the ship. *If it's true—totally worth it.*

❯ Ian Harrison, *Take Me to Your Leader* (Dorling Kindersley Ltd., 2007), 91.

Perhaps the most famous signal ever documented by the Search for Extraterrestrial Intelligence (SETI) was recorded at Ohio State University on August 15, 1977. Known as the "Wow!" signal, the transmission jumped from zero to thirty sigmas over the course of thirty-seven seconds and then faded away. Researches have tried for decades to capture the signal again, but to no avail. *If it really is aliens, probably best to pretend we're not home anyway.*

❯ Amir Alexander, "The Wow! Signal," *COSMOS* magazine, April 7, 2010, *www.cosmosmagazine.com.*

The Chicago Cubs have not played in the World Series since 1945. Many fans attribute this failure to the Curse of the Billy Goat, which was placed on the team by tavern keeper Billy Sianis when he was ejected from Wrigley Field for bringing his foul-smelling pet goat to the stadium. *It certainly doesn't have anything to do with the Cubs sucking.*

❯ Joshua Gee, *Encyclopedia Horrifica* (Scholastic, 2007), 116.

The rocks littering the ground at Racetrack Playa, Death Valley, may seem like ordinary pebbles; however, they are anything but. Many of the unassuming stones—some as heavy as eighty pounds—leave distinct trails in the earth that imply they have traveled hundreds of feet. Strangely enough, nobody has ever seen one move, and so far scientists can't explain how they do it. *It's just a game aliens play called "Let's make the scientists cry themselves to sleep."*

❯ Phillip F. Schewe, "Ice Offers Possible Explanation for Death Valley's Mysterious 'Self-Moving' Rocks," PhysOrg, February 17, 2011, *www.physorg.com.*

There are more UFO sightings and alleged alien encounters along Route 375 near Rachel, Nevada, than anywhere else in the world. The road is unofficially known as the UFO Highway. *Just because you get drunk and see something doesn't mean it exists.*

❯ Bill Geist, *Way Off the Road* (Broadway Books, 2007), 69.

The most commonly reported alien in America is the ubiquitous "gray," a creature that stands about three and a half feet tall with a gray body, large head, and disproportionately large eyes. *Little known fact: They give fabulous back rubs.*

❯ Jim Pipe, *Aliens (Tales of Horror)* (Bearport Publishing, August 2006), 10.

In response to a 2011 petition demanding the government reveal the truth about extraterrestrials, a senior White House official announced that the United States is not currently, nor has it ever been, in contact with alien beings. *Lies.*

> Deborah Netburn, "White House on Aliens: No Contact Yet, But We're Looking," *Los Angeles Times,* November 7, 2011, www.latimes.com.

Although billed as proof of the existence of mermaids, the infamous Feejee Mermaid displayed by P. T. Barnum was nothing more than an elaborate taxidermy of a monkey and a fish. *Maybe the ability to sew themselves together is what makes them magical?*

> Joshua Gee, Encyclopedia Horrifica (Scholastic, 2007), 17.

Scientists who advocate for the existence of Bigfoot speculate that at least 2,000 specimens walk the forests of North America. *Must be nice to be able to make up numbers and call yourself a scientist.*

> Stefan Lovgren, "Forensic Expert Says Bigfoot Is Real," *National Geographic,* October 23, 2003, www.news.national geographic.com.

Travelers in the Midwest may encounter stuffed specimens of the jackalope, a mysterious creature that resembles a cross between a pygmy deer and a rabbit. Believers insist it mimics the human voice to attract unsuspecting prey and its milk has medicinal properties. *It is also so imaginary that when it swings around 540 degrees, it becomes real.*

> Brenda Rosen, *The Mythical Creatures Bible: The Definitive Guide to Legendary Beings* (Sterling, March 3, 2009), 116.

In 2005, the Wyoming House of Representatives voted 45–12 to declare the jackalope the state's official mythical creature. The bill still sits with the state senate where it has been indefinitely postponed. *So close. Yet so far away.*

> ❯ "Jackalope Proposed as Wyoming's Official Mythical Creature," *Roadside America*, www.roadsideamerica.com.

A rabbit version of the HPV virus often causes sufferers to sprout horny growths from their skulls. Scientists believe this is the real basis for the jackalope myth. *Sounds like something a jackalope might say.*

> ❯ Emily Saarman, "How We Got the Controversial HPV Vaccine," Discover magazine, May 17, 2007, *www.discovermagazine .com.*

On May 19, 1780, a strange darkness slowly crept over New England. Residents had to read by candlelight at midday. There wasn't a cloud in the sky, and there was no eclipse on that day. The mysterious shroud has never been explained. *My guess: Early red-headed Americans trying to destroy their single greatest enemy.*

> ❯ Phyllis Goldman, *Monkeyshines on Strange and Wonderful Facts* (Monkeyshines, 1991), 12.

After the 2002 death of Bigfoot researcher Raymond Wallace, his children revealed he had made the whole thing up. He staged his elaborate hoax by using a pair of large wooden feet to stamp a trail of footprints in a California logging camp in 1958. *Nice try, but I'm not buying it. Bigfoot is just as real as you, me, and the little gnomes that live in my sock drawer.*

> ❯ Timothy Egan, "Search for Bigfoot Outlives the Man Who Created Him," *The New York Times,* January 3, 2003, *www.nytimes.com.*

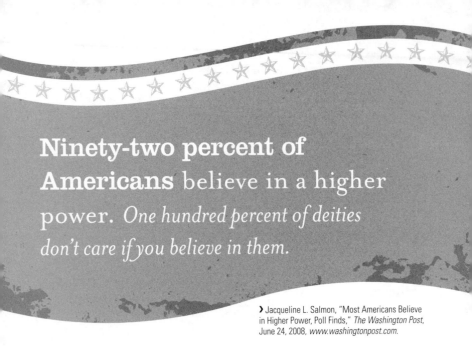

Ninety-two percent of Americans believe in a higher power. *One hundred percent of deities don't care if you believe in them.*

> Jacqueline L. Salmon, "Most Americans Believe in Higher Power, Poll Finds," *The Washington Post*, June 24, 2008, *www.washingtonpost.com*.

Despite popular belief to the contrary, the SETI Institute does not receive any government money to conduct its searches. It receives all of its funding through private donations. *Not sure if that makes their failures more or less understandable.*

> "Our Mission," SETI Institute, *www.seti.org*.

The Federal Aviation Administration urges citizens to contact a toll-free number dedicated for reporting UFO sightings at 1-877-979-7444. You can also e-mail them at *reporting@baass.org*. *Please use that information irresponsibly.*

> "Section 6. Safety, Accident, and Hazard Reports," Federal Aviation Administration, *www.faa.gov*.

Three rules governed American expeditions searching Nepal for the Abominable Snowman. The first rule required the expeditions purchase a permit, while the second insisted adventurers refrain from killing the beast if at all possible. The third rule stated that any news of the existence of the creature must be cleared through the Nepalese government. *Rule Four: Enhanced interrogation techniques can be used only if the Yeti appears to have knowledge as to the location of Santa Claus.*

❯ Paul Bedard and Lauren Fox, "Documents Show Feds Believed in the Yeti," *U.S. News & World Report*, September 2, 2011, *www.usnews.com.*

Actress Tallulah Bankhead was buried with a lucky rabbit's foot given to her by her father. *Or an unknown rabbit is buried with his unlucky human.*

❯ Varla Ventura, *Beyond Bizarre: Frightening Facts and Blood-Curdling True Tales* (Weiser Books, 2010).

In September 2000, a group of researchers prepared a plaster cast of a depression they believe was created by a Bigfoot lounging in the Skookum Meadows in Washington State. The Skookum cast weighs 400 pounds. Analysts speculate the dimensions of the animal are roughly 40 to 50 percent larger than a normal human. *So a really fat guy went for a hike, got tired, and lay down. Case closed.*

❯ Stefan Lovgren, "Forensic Expert Says Bigfoot Is Real," *National Geographic*, October 23, 2003, *www.news.national geographic.com.*

Vertically challenged visitors to Gold Hill, Oregon, can look forward to a sudden boost in stature—albeit temporarily. The town is home to the Oregon Vortex, a strange site that makes individuals appear taller or shorter, depending on where they stand. *So I can be taller, but I have to stand in Oregon forever? Tough call.*

❯ Sarah Kershaw, "Tourist Draw for Sale, with Mystery the Lure," *The New York Times*, September 19, 2003, *www.nytimes.com.*

On October 1, 1948, World War II veteran George F. Gorman claimed he participated in a game of chicken with a small blinking orb of light in the skies above Fargo, North Dakota. The orb moved faster than any plane he'd encountered and flew straight at him before breaking off at the last minute on two separate occasions. When Gorman landed, a Geiger counter revealed slightly elevated levels of radiation surrounding his plane. *So aliens are fast, daring, and radioactive, with a flair for the dramatic. Super.*

❯ Seth Foreman, "5 UFO Sightings That Even Non-Crazy People Find Creepy," *Cracked*, August 9, 2010. *www.cracked.com.*

The home of University of California–San Diego Chancellor Marye Anne Fox rests atop a Native American burial ground. *Sort of like* Cujo, *but thirty-three times less exciting.*

❯ Eleanor Yang Su, "Regents OK Fox's Housing Exception, $20,000 Allowance," Sign on San Diego, March 25, 2010, *www.signonsandiego.com.*

Although experts insist it was actually Venus, former president Jimmy Carter believes he saw an alien spacecraft while attending a Lion's Club Meeting in 1969. *Sort of like the time I saw a leprechaun that turned out to just be a short, fat kid.*

❯ Dane Sherwood, Sandy Wood, and Kara Kovalchik, *The Pocket Idiot's Guide to Not So Useless Facts* (Penguin Group, 2006), 42.

The Integration Chamber in Giant Rock, California reportedly has the ability to reverse the aging process. The domed structure was built in 1978 by George Van Tassel and bombards visitors with a series of sounds set at certain frequencies that allegedly rejuvenate guests who stand within the "sound bath." *Sure it does.*

❯ Eric Peterson, "4 Paranormal and Other Strange Roadside Attractions," The Learning Channel, *www.tlc.howstuffworks.com.*

One in five Americans believe in the existence of witches. *That sounds suspiciously like something a witch would say.*

> David W. Moore, "Three in Four Americans Believe in Paranormal," Gallup, June 16, 2005, *www.gallup.com.*

The James Randi Educational Foundation holds $1 million in an investment account ready to be awarded to any individual who can demonstrate a legitimate paranormal ability. So far, nobody has claimed the prize. *That's just because they refuse to acknowledge a butt-cheek symphony as "paranormal."*

> Sadie Crabtree, "JREF's $1,000,000 Paranormal Challenge Now Easier Than Ever," James Randi Educational Foundation, March 9, 2011, *www .randi.org.*

Four out of five Americans believe the United States government possesses intimate knowledge of extraterrestrials but is hiding that information from the public. *That's just what the aliens want you to think.*

> Robert Todd Carroll, *The Skeptic's Dictionary: A Collection of Strange Beliefs, Amusing Deceptions, and Dangerous Delusions* (John Wiley and Sons, 2003), 10.

On September 25, 2004, Mayor Ron Garitone proudly declared his city, Wallace, Idaho, as the undisputed center of the universe—specifically, the intersection of Bank Street and Sixth Street. His logic? You can't prove it isn't true. *That's the same reasoning my brother used to claim I was adopted.*

> "Center of the Universe," Historic Wallace Idaho, *www.wallace-id.com.*

Sitting atop Wyoming's Big Horn Mountain is a series of rocks arranged in an uneven circle roughly eighty feet across. Likely constructed by the Plains Indians and known as "the medicine wheel," the structure confuses archaeologists. No one is quite sure what purpose the circle served. *The elders said it would keep out the White Man. The elders were wrong.*

> Phyllis Goldman, *Monkeyshines on Strange and Wonderful Facts* (Monkeyshines, 1991), 16.

The Jersey Devil was originally known as the Leed's Devil, in reference to the Leeds Point, New Jersey, woman who supposedly gave birth to the cursed creature in 1735. *The Jersey Devil is just a misunderstanding. Has anyone ever seen a baby born in New Jersey? They're all hideous.*

> Loren Coleman and Jerome Clark, *Cryptozoology A To Z: The Encyclopedia of Loch Monsters, Sasquatch, Chupacabras, and Other Authentic Mysteries of Nature* (Fireside, 1999), 120.

Actors Bill Murray and Dan Aykroyd have only reprised their roles as ghostbusters on one occasion since filming the movies: to visit a terminally ill child who wanted to meet them. *The kid was fine until they crossed the streams.*

> "Dan Aykroyd," IMDb, *www.imdb.com*.

Missouri residents tell tales of Old Raw Head, the reanimated corpse of a magical hog with the fangs of a panther, the claws of a bear, and the tail of a raccoon. According to legend, every Halloween the monster stalks the Ozark Mountains searching for his killer. *The more I read that, the less I want to hang out with people from Missouri.*

> Richard Young and Judy Dockrey Young, *Favorite Scary Stories of American Children* (August House, 1989), 11.

One-third of Americans
believe aliens have visited earth.
The rest are clearly aliens.

❯ Jessica Williams, *50 Facts That Should Change the World 2.0* (The Disinformation Company, 2007), 124.

The CIA estimates that more than half of all UFO sightings reported during the fifties and sixties were due to U-2 and SR-71 spy planes. *The rest were totally aliens though.*

❯ Phil Patton, "6 Top-Secret Aircraft That Are Mistaken for UFOs," *Popular Mechanics*, February 18, 2009, *www.popularmechanics.com*.

The American munitions manufacturer Hornady markets a line of bullets specifically for use on the undead called "Zombie Max." *There are 7 billion people on this planet. You will run out of bullets way before you run out of zombies.*

❯ "Zombie Max," *Hornady*, www.hornady.com.

Sightings of strange hairless creatures with leathery heads and wide, lipless mouths have been reported near the Little Miami River in Loveland, Ohio, dating back to the 1950s. These three-foot-tall Frog People are most often sighted late at night and tend to flee into the water when sighted. *They also taste like chicken. Don't ask how I know.*

❯ "Frog People," *Roadside America,* www.roadsideamerica .com.

On July 25, 1977, Ruth Lowe of Lawndale, Illinois, and seven other witnesses watched as two giant birds swooped down from the sky and carried her ten-year-old son several feet before dropping him and disappearing. Many cryptozoologists cite this event as definitive proof that massive birds of prey dubbed "Thunderbirds" stalk the skies across the United States. *They are exceptionally good at hiding behind clouds.*

❯ Loren Coleman and Jerome Clark, *Cryptozoology A To Z: The Encyclopedia of Loch Monsters, Sasquatch, Chupacabras, and Other Authentic Mysteries of Nature* (Fireside, 1999), 134.

In 1968, an injured Honolulu hospital patient informed his nurse he would need to leave for a while that evening to visit his alien friend aboard a UFO. When the staff checked the beds that night, the patient (who was unable to walk and confined to his bed) was nowhere to be found. After much searching, they returned to the room to find him lying in traction, just as he was when he made his calm announcement hours earlier. *They were actually more acquaintances than friends.*

❯ Phyllis Goldman, *Monkeyshines on Strange and Wonderful Facts* (Monkeyshines, 1991), 11.

On August 22, 1924, the planet Mars was closer to Earth than it had been in more than 100 years. Using the event as an opportunity to listen for potential alien broadcasts, many radio stations instituted a "National Radio Silence Day," where they ceased broadcasting for a few minutes every hour. *Think of it this way: If you were an alien, would you contact us?*

> ❯ Keith Cowing, "Government-Sponsored SETI—in the 1920s," NASA Watch, November 8, 2009, *www.nasawatch.com.*

The island of Oahu in Hawaii contains one of the world's only backward waterfalls. Powerful updrafts blow the water up into the air, giving the appearance that the water defies gravity. *To answer your unasked question: Yes, if you pee into the falls, your pee will become magical.*

> ❯ Phyllis Goldman, *Monkeyshines on Strange and Wonderful Facts* (Monkeyshines, 1991), 9.

Outside a courthouse in Crossville, Tennessee, sits a statue of the Flying Spaghetti Monster, the deity of the farcical Pastafarian religion, which was started to protest the teaching of intelligent design in public schools. *I'm pretty sure that violates the separation of church and state. Sort of.*

> ❯ Daniel Terdiman, "Flying Spaghetti Monster Statue at Tennessee Courthouse," CNet, March 31, 2008, *www.news.cnet.com.*

In 2005, the popular website Boing Boing offered a $250,000 prize—later raised to $1 million—to anyone who could provide empirical evidence that Jesus was not the son of the Flying Spaghetti Monster. Nobody has claimed the money. Yet. *Because the Bible told me so. Now give me my money!*

> ❯ Xeni Jardin, "Boing Boing's $250,000 Intelligent Design Challenge," Boing Boing, August 19, 2005, *www.boingboing.net.*

According to a Gallup poll, 42 percent of Americans believe that "people on this earth are sometimes possessed by the devil." Unfortunately, the poll did not determine whether those responders meant literally, or figuratively. *Trust me, they meant literally.*

> David W. Moore, "Three in Four Americans Believe in Paranormal," Gallup, June 16, 2005, *www.gallup.com.*

Vermont's minor league baseball team is called "The Vermont Lake Monsters" as a tribute to the famed aquatic cryptid, Champ. *Vermont: Where the most interesting thing about the state isn't even real.*

> "Vermont Lake Monsters," MiLB.com, *www.minorleague baseball.com.*

In 1972, American astronomer J. Allen Hynek outlined the types of encounters one might have with aliens. Viewing an alien spacecraft from a distance defines the first kind, while discovering alien debris or other evidence and actually sighting an alien creature define the second and third kinds. *What kind is it if two aliens have sex with a honey badger while I watch?*

> Jim Pipe, *Aliens (Tales of Horror)* (Bearport Publishing, 2006), 8.

Although it was never revealed in the popular television series *Lost*, the "Smoke Monster" was actually named "Barry." *Yet they can't explain where the polar bears came from?*

> Kristin Dos Santos, "Lost: Want to Know the Man in Black's Real Name?" E! Online, May 24, 2010, *www.eonline .com.*

❧ CHAPTER 4 ❧

Would You Like Fries with Your Bull Testicles?

Weird American Delicacies to Gross You Out

If there's one thing Americans love to do, it's eat. And not just ordinary things like deep-fried butter and 1,400-pound wheels of cheese, but weird stuff too. I've personally never wondered what jellied moose nose tastes like, but apparently Mainers love the stuff.

Whether you are a connoisseur of fermented salmon heads, or you have a soft spot in your heart for "Rocky Mountain oysters," all of the stomach-churning secrets of the American culinary scene are just a page-turn away.

For a brief time in the 1940s, the U.S. government considered butter and margarine to be the seventh essential food group. *"Now kids, eat your butter logs or you won't get any ice cream."*

> Peter Granitz, "Butter and Margarine: the Seventh Food Group," NPR, August 23, 2011, *www.npr.org.*

Bubble gum is traditionally pink because it was the only color on hand when inventor Walter Diemer perfected the recipe. *And because pink is the tastiest color.*

> "Fun Facts," Better Oral Health, *www.betteroralhealth.info.*

During the 1893 World's Fair held in Chicago, concessionaire Anton Feuchtwanger could not convince fairgoers to try his Bavarian piping hot sausages. He even offered up gloves to protect the hands of customers, with little success. In the end, he tried serving the sausages tucked into a long bun and the American hot dog was born. *And so began our country's obsession with obesity.*

> Arkady Leokum and K. R. Hobbie, *The Little Giant Book of Weird & Wacky Facts* (Sterling Publishing Company, 2005), 20.

Washington state produces 40 percent of the world's hops. *And 80 percent of the world's hipsters.*

> John Wilnes, "Washington State Hops Dominate World Production," Workforce Explorer, August 3, 2007, *www.work forceexplorer.com*

To keep cool during games, Babe Ruth kept a cabbage leaf under his hat and changed it every two innings. *And yes, he ate it.*

❯ "The Discovernator," Discovery Channel, *www.news.discovery.com.*

To scare citizens away from drinking illicit alcohol during Prohibition, the U.S. government poisoned large shipments of industrial alcohol that were typically stolen by bootleggers and resold. Some experts estimate as many as 10,000 Americans died as a result. *And you think you have it rough when the government cuts Medicaid.*

❯ Deborah Blum, "The Chemist's War," *Slate*, February 19, 2010, *www.slate.com.*

Almost half of Americans don't realize that white bread is made from wheat. *Apparently "white" is not a legitimate ingredient.*

❯ Noel Botham, *The Mega Book of Useless Information* (John Blake, 2009), 336.

Residents of the Midwest eat nearly double the number of frozen pizzas of most Americans. *Are they fat because they eat more frozen pizza, or do they eat more frozen pizza because they're fat?*

> Luke Meredith and Hillary Rhodes, "Midwest Is the U.S. Frozen Pizza Capital—Nobody Knows Why," *Lubbock Avalanche-Journal*, August 21, 2007, www.lubbockonline.com.

The FDA allows for an average of nineteen maggots per 100 grams of canned mushrooms. This number drops to five if the maggots are 2 millimeters or longer. *At first I thought it shouldn't matter how big the maggots are. Then I thought about eating ten tiny maggots versus one huge one and realized it absolutely does.*

> "Food Defect Action Levels," U.S. Food and Drug Administration Center for Food Safety and Applied Nutrition, July 2011, www.fda.gov/food/guidancecomplianceregulatory information/guidancedocuments/sanitation/ucm056174.htm.

The signature drink of the Sourdough Saloon in Dawson City, Alaska, is called the "Sourtoe Cocktail," and consists of a shot of the customer's favorite hard alcohol served in a glass along with a dehydrated human toe. *Bottoms up.*

> David Moye, "'Sourtoe Cocktail': Father and Son Bond Over Drinking Dead Man's Toe," *The Huffington Post*, November 3, 2011, www.huffingtonpost.com.

In 2006, Florida middle schooler Jasmine Roberts took ice samples from several local fast-food restaurants and compared it to the toilet water found in the same establishments. In 70 percent of the samples, the ice contained more bacteria than the toilet water. *What you're eating can barely be defined as food. I wouldn't worry about the ice in your cup.*

> "Fast-Food Ice Dirtier Than Toilet Water," ABC News, February 20, 2006, www.abcnews.go.com.

The prize for single most-caloric American food belongs to the Aussie Cheese Fries with Ranch Dressing served at Outback Steakhouse. The dish contains an artery-clogging 2,900 calories and 182 grams of fat. *Challenge accepted.*

> ❯ Matt Goulding, "The 20 Worst Foods in America," *Men's Health, www.menshealth.com.*

In 2008, lawyers for Procter & Gamble successfully avoided a 17.5 percent tax in the United Kingdom on their popular Pringles snack by arguing that the product was not actually a chip. According to the company a Pringle is only about 42 percent potato. *Come on, you knew something was up. Nothing that delicious can be legit.*

> ❯ Carey Alexander, "Procter & Gamble: Pringles Are Not Potato Chips," *The Consumerist*, July 5, 2008, *www.consumerist.com.*

In 1972, the Gerber Products company tried to market puréed meals for adults served in jars similar to their popular baby food products. Dubbed "Gerber Singles," the product never caught on. *Contrary to popular belief, apparently starving college students won't eat everything.*

> ❯ "10 Foods That (Thankfully) Flopped," Mental Floss, November 21, 2009, *www.mentalfloss .com.*

In the early 1800s, the mint julep rivaled coffee as the preferred morning pick-me-up in the American South. *Could explain why the North won.*

> ❯ Dane Sherwood, Sandy Wood, and Kara Kovalchik, *The Pocket Idiot's Guide to Not So Useless Facts* (Penguin Group, 2006).

The FDA allows an average of 225 insect fragments or 4.5 rodent hairs per 8 ounces of macaroni or noodle products. *Don't complain. Even without the pasta, that's almost a full meal right there.*

❯ JoNel Aleccia, "A Second Chance for Faulty Food? FDA Calls It 'Reconditioning,'" MSNBC, November 23, 2011, *www.msnbc.msn.com.*

The meat in one hamburger can come from as many as 100 different cows. *Each one more delicious than the last.*

❯ Ari Solomon, "One Hundred Animals in a Bun," *The Huffington Post,* August 13, 2010, *www.huffingtonpost.com.*

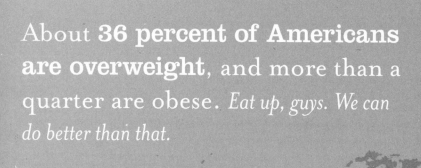

About **36 percent of Americans are overweight**, and more than a quarter are obese. *Eat up, guys. We can do better than that.*

❯ Bill Hendrick, "Percentage of Overweight, Obese Americans Swells," WebMD, February 10, 2010, *www.webmd.com.*

One out of four Americans eat fast food every single day. *Good health is overrated anyway. You can't eat good health.*

> "Americans Are Obsessed with Fast Food: the Dark Side of the All-American Meal," CBS News, February 11, 2009, *www.cbsnews.com.*

Milton S. Hershey, founder of Hershey Chocolate, purchased a $300 ticket aboard the *Titanic* but avoided the fateful voyage due to a scheduling conflict. *Evidence that God loves us and wants us to eat chocolate.*

> "10 People Who Did Not Board the Titanic," Listverse, December 9, 2011, *www.listverse.com.*

Livestock receive 80 percent of the antibiotics sold in the United States. *Got to make sure they're healthy before we start hacking away.*

> Maryn Mckenna, "Update: Farm Animals Get 80 Percent of Antibiotics Sold in U.S.," *Wired*, December 24, 2010, *www.wired.com.*

In 1959 the FDA discovered traces of the weedkiller aminotriazole in a shipment of cranberries from Oregon. Citizens panicked and refused to purchase the fruit. In an attempt to end the panic, President John F. Kennedy gulped down two glasses of cranberry juice while posing for pictures. *He made Marilyn try it first though. Just to be safe.*

> Thomas McAdam, "Famous Health Scares: the Great Cranberry Scare of 1959," Examiner.com, June 17, 2009, *www.examiner.com.*

If you purchased a single share of Coca-Cola stock in 1919 when the company first went public, seventy-six years later you could have sold it for $92,500. *Hindsight is very expensive.*

❯ Noel Botham, *The Bumper Book of Useless Information* (John Blake, April 2008), 202.

The Delaware-based brewery Dogfish

Head produces a beer using ingredients from every continent on earth. *How very un–American of them.*

❯ "Pangea," Dogfish Head, *www.dogfish.com.*

For a shipment of frozen broccoli to be considered unfit for sale, it must contain an average of sixty or more aphids and/or thrips and/or mites per 100 grams. *I don't know what a thrip is, but I sure as hell don't want it in my broccoli.*

❯ "Food Defect Action Levels," U.S. Food and Drug Administration Center for Food Safety and Applied Nutrition, July 2011, *www.fda.gov.*

People for the Ethical Treatment of Animals (PETA) offers a $1 million prize for anyone who can develop a way to grow animal meat in a laboratory, thus bypassing the need to slaughter animals. *I long for a future where I can grow my own bacon.*

❯ "PETA Offers $1 Million Reward to First to Make In Vitro Meat," People for the Ethical Treatment of Animals, *www.peta.org.*

The graham cracker was originally invented by Reverend Sylvester Graham, a Connecticut Presbyterian minister who hoped the crackers—combined with a vegetarian diet—would curb the sex drive of his parishioners. *I see the mouthful of crackers as more of a challenge than a deterrent.*

❯ "Polly Adler Want a Cracker," Snopes, *www.snopes.com.*

After federal prisons banned smoking in 2004, inmates turned to packages of mackerel as a new form of currency. They use the oily fish to pay for everything from haircuts to homebrewed booze. *I seriously couldn't make that up if I tried.*

❯ Justin Scheck, "Mackerel Economics in Prison Leads to Appreciation for Oily Fillets," *The Wall Street Journal,* October 2, 2008, *www.wsj.com.*

Any food that does not arrive at the White House in designated delivery trucks is promptly destroyed. Even Girl Scout cookies. *I shall have to consider a plan B for "Operation Give the President Food Poisoning So He Gets Really Sick and Is Super Upset About It."*

❯ "Mrs. Stamberg's Relish Goes to Washington," NPR, November 18, 2011, *www.npr.org.*

In 1973, Southwest Airlines offered customers the option of either a $13 fare from Dallas to Houston or a bottle of premium liquor with the purchase of a full-fare $26 ticket. The promotion made Southwest the largest distributor in Texas of Chivas, Crown Royal, and Smirnoff for the following two months. *If given the option, always choose booze. It tastes much better than money.*

❯ "1972 to 1978 Luv Over Texas," Southwest Media, *www.swamedia.com.*

Out of every ten ears of corn grown in the United States, only two are sold for human consumption. The rest are used as animal feed and to produce ethanol gasoline. *If it was all hothouse corn, this wouldn't be an issue.*

> Chris Keenan, "Americans Now Use More Corn for Fuel Than Food," Gas2, October 17, 2011, *www.gas2.org.*

In 1919, a fifty-foot-high steel tank filled with 2.5 million gallons of molasses burst in Boston's North End, sending a colossal wave of sticky liquid streaming through the city's streets. The wave killed twenty-one people and injured an additional 150. *If you can't outrun molasses, it's your own fault.*

> "Frequently Asked Questions," The Massachusetts Historical Society, *www.masshist.org.*

In 2008, Burger King started marketing a men's body spray called Flame. The fragrance was designed to make the wearer smell like the chain's popular flame-broiled Whopper sandwich. *It is also a great, noninvasive birth control method.*

> Sarika Dani, "Appetite for Seduction: BK's New Fragrance," MSNBC, December 17, 2008, *www.today.msnbc.msn.com.*

At the behest of the FDA, tap water is tested for contaminants hundreds of times every month. The EPA only requires bottled water manufacturers to test their water once a week. *It may not be as clean, but water tastes better when I know it will kill a seagull when I'm done with it.*

> Josh Peterson, "Which is Healthier: Tap Water or Bottled Water?," Planet Green, April 27, 2009, *www.planetgreen .discovery.com.*

About 70 percent of Chuck E. Cheese restaurants serve alcohol, a fact many feel contributes to the disproportionate number of times police are called to the company's numerous locations, as opposed to other family restaurants. *It's not really a birthday party until daddy takes off his shirt and piledrives an eight-year-old for hogging Big Buck Hunter.*

❯ Anna Prior, "Calling All Cars: Trouble at Chuck E. Cheese's, Again," *The Wall Street Journal*, December 9, 2008, *www.wsj.com*.

Every hour, approximately **800,000 chickens** are killed for food in the United States. Or, about 7 billion a year. *It's their own fault for being so delicious.*

❯ "Chickens Used for Food," PETA, *www.peta.org*.

Castoreum, an FDA-approved substance obtained from the sex glands of beavers, is a commonly found ingredient in products ranging from perfumes and medicine to drinks and desserts. However, it is usually listed simply as "natural flavorings." *Joke's on you, hippies. I only eat processed food.*

❯ "Natural Flavors & Castoreum," Gentle World, *www.gentleworld.org*.

Chop Suey, one of the most popular dishes served at Chinese food restaurants in America, is not Chinese at all. It was actually invented in California. *My whole life has been based on a lie.*

❯ Nancy Shute, "In Praise of Chop Suey," *U.S. News World Report*, August 7, 2005, *www.usnews.com*.

The average American's cutting board contains over 200 times more fecal coliforms than the average toilet. *Just extra flavor.*

❯ Danielle Braff, "Eliminate Germs in Your Home," *Men's Health, www.menshealth.com.*

For every forty-five days at sea, each U.S. navy vessel is permitted to provide crew members with a "beer day," whereby each sailor receives two beers. *Luckily, "black tar heroin day" only comes once every five years.*

❯ Shuana Garbiack, "Kearsarge Gets 1st Break—Heads Home," United States Navy, June 9, 2003, *www.navy.mil.*

Ground cinnamon can contain ten or more rodent hairs per 50 grams and still pass inspection.

Just think of it as kissing a rat every time you bake.

❯ "Food Defect Action Levels," U.S. Food and Drug Administration Center for Food Safety and Applied Nutrition, July 2011, *www.fda.gov.*

Despite their aquatic namesake, Rocky Mountain oysters are actually bull testicles that have been peeled, pounded flat, dredged in flour, and then fried in oil. The dish is served as an appetizer and is quite popular in the western part of the United States. *Reason 2,372 never to cross the Mississippi.*

❯ John Mitzewich, "Rocky Mountain Oysters," About.com, *www.about.com.*

The record for Rocky Mountain oyster eating belongs to competitive eater Pat "Deep Dish" Bertoletti. In August 2010 at a Colorado casino, Bertoletti choked down three pounds, 11.75 ounces of the deep-fried delights in a mere ten minutes to win the $1,500 first prize. *Not nearly enough cash to justify eating almost four pounds of balls.*

❯ Lynn Debruin, "Man Eats 4 lbs. of Yummy 'Oysters,'" ESPN, August 31, 2010, *www.sports.espn.go.com.*

In 2001, the Pentagon was forced to change the color of food aid packages being dropped over Afghanistan when they realized—much to their horror—that the yellow packages shared a color and shape with another far less benevolent object—unexploded cluster bombs. *In their defense, the people who initially decided on yellow were really, really dumb.*

❯ Times Wire Services, "Food Aid Packets in Search of a Color," *Los Angeles Times*, November 3, 2001, *www.latimes.com.*

For every **100 grams of peanut butter**, the FDA allows thirty insect fragments. *Meh. Bonus protein.*

❯ "Top 10 Incredible Food Facts," Listverse.com, December 17, 2007, *www.listverse.com.*

Each reintroduction of the McRib sandwich has directly coincided with a drop in the price of pork. *Mmmmm, discount pork.*

❯ Daniel Hamermesh, "The Marginal Cost of the McRib," Freakonomics, December 1, 2011, *www.freakonomics.com.*

In 1969, a storm of mildly sweet white powder started falling over Chester, South Carolina. Residents traced the strange meteorological phenomenon to a nearby Borden, Inc. factory. Whenever the exhaust vents at the plant became clogged, traces of a new corn syrup–based nondairy creamer spewed out into the atmosphere. *Most delicious storm ever.*

❯ David Wallechinsky, *The Book Of Lists: The Original Compendium of Curious Information* (Canongate Books, 2009).

In 1835, Colonel Thomas S. Meacham sent President Andrew Jackson a 1,400-pound wheel of cheese as a gift. Unable to consume it himself, the president offered it to guests at his last public White House reception, and they devoured it in a scant two hours. *Never underestimate the appeal of free cheese.*

❯ Chris Good, "Picture of the Day: Andrew Jackson's Giant Wheel of Cheese," *The Atlantic*, March 3, 2011, *www.theatlantic.com.*

Economists can (and occasionally do) use the price of a Big Mac in a particular country to accurately gauge the value of its currency. The resulting information is known as the Big Mac Index.
No matter how weak the U.S. dollar becomes, rest assured the Big Mac will always remain strong.

❯ "Currency Comparisons, To Go," *The Economist*, July 28, 2011, *www.economist.com.*

In 1931, White Castle funded a study that examined the effect living on nothing but White Castle Sliders for thirteen weeks might have on a lone medical student. By all accounts, the student remained in good health. *Not dying from eating something does not make it good for you.*

❭ "Fun Facts," White Castle, *www.whitecastle.com.*

The popsicle was invented in 1905 by eleven-year-old Frank Epperson. During an unusually cold San Francisco night, Epperson left a mixture of powdered soda and water on a porch and discovered a delicious treat waiting for him the next morning. Eighteen years later, he filed a patent for his creation. *Not the brightest bulb in the box if it took him eighteen years to perfect frozen soda.*

❭ "Top 10 Incredible Food Facts," Listverse.com, December 17, 2007, *www.listverse.com.*

A ripe cranberry will bounce. *Not very helpful if you intend to eat it afterward.*

❭ *National Geographic Kids, Weird but True! 3: 300 Outrageous Facts* (National Geographic Children's Books, 2011), 42.

Because chocolate and grease are potentially damaging to puppets, the "cookies" consumed by the Cookie Monster on Sesame Street are actually rice cakes decorated to look like cookies. *Now we know who the real monsters are.*

❭ "Muppets Cookie Monster," ABC For Kids, *www.abc.net.au.*

Coca-Cola is available in more countries than there are in the United Nations. *Saving the world, one cavity at a time.*

❯ "Coca-Cola Featured on *National Geographic* Channel's Ultimate Factories Series," Coca-Cola, *www.thecoca-cola company.com*.

When it was first invented in 1920, the popular soft drink 7UP contained small amounts of Lithium, a drug used to treat bipolar disorder. *Pity the FDA frowns upon that sort of thing now.*

❯ Jamie Frater, *Listverse.com's Ultimate Book of Bizarre Lists: Fascinating Facts and Shocking Trivia on Movies, Music, Crime, Celebrities, History, and More* (Ulysses Press, 2010), 164.

Often referred to as "stink heads," fermented salmon heads are a traditional Alaskan dish. After the fish are caught, the heads are removed and buried for several weeks before they are dug up, mashed into a pudding, and served cold. *Remember, kids, eating rotten fish doesn't make you cool. It makes you an idiot.*

❯ Ryan Lawrence, "Top 10 Most Gross & Disgusting Food" Toptenz, *www.toptenz.net*.

If you are standing in the continental United States, you are never more than 145 miles from a McDonald's restaurant. *Resistance is futile.*

❯ "Map of Every McDonald's in the Country," Good, September 24, 2009, *www.good.is*.

Richard Nixon's favorite lunch consisted of cottage cheese and ketchup. *See, hippies, he didn't eat babies.*

> "Mrs. Stamberg's Relish Goes to Washington," NPR, November 18, 2011, *www.npr.org.*

The Algonquian Indians called Chicago "Chicagoua" or "onion place." *Only because there was no word for "The land where dwell the assholes with guns."*

> Mike Bellino, *Fun Food Facts* (AuthorHouse, 2008), 56.

Every year, the inhabitants of Hawaii consume more than six million cans of SPAM. *Self destruction: the official pastime of our off-shore brothers and sisters.*

> "Hawaii's Love Affair with Canned Item Continues," *Today,* February 22, 2009, *www.today .msnbc.msn.com.*

At San Francisco's Opaque restaurant, customers learn to experience their meal with all their senses—save their eyes. The restaurant is kept in a state of complete and total darkness. A team of visually impaired wait staff services customers by touch. *Skipping out on a bill has never been so simultaneously easy and impossible.*

❯ Amanda Gold, "What's New: Dining in the Dark—Literally—at Opaque in San Francisco," *San Francisco Chronicle*, June 25, 2008, *www.sfgate.com.*

The FDA allows companies to use the term "light" on any product that has a history of carrying the word, regardless of the nutritional content. *So light Twinkies, not so much?*

❯ "Make Healthier Choices by Knowing What Labels Like Low Fat and Light Really Mean," Lifehacker, *www.lifehacker.com.*

Since the early 1990s, municipal waste-water plants across the country have been selling "sewer sludge" to farmers to use as fertilizer for crops later sold in grocery stores. *So there's a chance, albeit a small one, that you've eaten my poop.*

❯ "Sewage Sludge," Center For Food Safety, *www.centerfor foodsafety.org.*

The average American teen consumes thirty-four teaspoons of sugar a day. *Solution: free insulin shots with every can of soda.*

❯ Associated Press, "Cut Back, Way Back, on Sugar, Says Heart Group," MSNBC, August 24, 2009, *www.msnbc.msn.com.*

To prove that dieting success is all about calorie restriction, Kansas State University nutrition professor Mark Haub spent ten weeks in 2010 eating about 1,800 calories of Twinkies, powdered donuts, Doritos, and sugary cereal every day. He lost twenty-seven pounds. *Some call him professor. I call him Hero.*

> Madison Park, "Twinkie Diet Helps Nutrition Professor Lose 27 Pounds," CNN, November 8, 2010, *www.cnn.com.*

Popular mostly in Alaska and parts of Maine, jellied moose nose consists of the upper jaw of a moose that has been boiled, picked clean of hairs, then simmered with herbs and spices and allowed to cool and congeal. The dish is served chilled and sliced. *Still only half as gross as a Slim Jim.*

> Ryan Lawrence, "Top 10 Most Gross & Disgusting Food" Toptenz, *www.toptenz.net.*

Despite popular belief to the contrary, the **Hydrox cookie** was invented four years before the Oreo. *The best cookie is the one closest to your mouth.*

> Christopher Rhoads, "The Hydrox Cookie Is Dead, and Fans Won't Get Over It," *The Wall Street Journal,* January 19, 2008, *www.wsj.com.*

After the appearance of the *Popeye* cartoon in 1931, spinach consumption skyrocketed by 33 percent in the United States. *And the level of grumpiness among the nation's youth increased 1,000 percent.*

> Noel Botham, *The Bumper Book of Useless Information* (John Blake, April 2008), 344.

Although popular in Chinese restaurants, the fortune cookie was invented in San Francisco at the Japanese Tea Garden. *Fortune cookies also cause Alzheimer's. Every time I eat one, it's because I forgot how disgusting they are.*

> Dane Sherwood, Sandy Wood, and Kara Kovalchik, *The Pocket Idiot's Guide to Not So Useless Facts* (Penguin Group, 2006), 46.

In 2005, a startling number of individuals filed second prize claims for a Powerball drawing. Lottery officials suspected fraud, but all the claims for between $100,000 and $500,000 were legitimate—the 110 contestants all played the same numbers from fortune cookies. *Which is why I distribute fortune cookies that read: "Give all your worldly possessions to Eric Grzymkowski."*

> "Fortune Cookie Fortune," Snopes, *www.snopes.com*.

A hot dog can last more than twenty years in a landfill. *Well, do you want your food to be delicious or biodegradable?*

> *National Geographic Kids, Weird But True: 300 Outrageous Facts* (*National Geographic* Children's Books, 2009), 33.

Marlon Brando was famous for his love of food. It was not uncommon for him to consume two whole chickens, half a cheesecake, and a pint of ice cream in a single sitting. He once created his own Mounds Bar—sort of—by cracking open a coconut, melting some chocolate in the sun, and then stirring it into the coconut. *The man was a genius!*

> Jerome Litt, MD, "Marlon Brando Was a Binge Eater," *Psychology Today*, September 3, 2009, *www.psychologytoday.com*.

The term "brain freeze" was invented by 7-Eleven to refer to the pain experienced when indulging in a Slurpee too quickly. The medical term is "sphenopalatine ganglioneuralgia." *The medical community needs to stop stringing random letters together and calling them names.*

> Jamie Frater, *Listverse.com's Ultimate Book of Bizarre Lists: Fascinating Facts and Shocking Trivia on Movies, Music, Crime, Celebrities, History, and More* (Ulysses Press, 2010), 163.

The strings on boxes of Barnum's Animal Crackers are in place so customers can hang them from Christmas trees. *They also make it easier to taunt your friends at snack time.*

> Dane Sherwood, Sandy Wood, and Kara Kovalchik, *The Pocket Idiot's Guide to Not So Useless Facts* (Penguin Group, 2006), 45.

Despite indisputable evidence suggesting tomatoes are a fruit, there are many who insist they are in fact vegetables. This is because in 1893, the U.S. Supreme Court defined vegetables as "plant foods served in, with, or after the soup, fish, or meat" for tax purposes. *The tomato may not actually be the New Jersey state vegetable, but the fact that Jerseyites have thought about designating it as such is equally upsetting.*

> Glen Vecchione, Joel Harris, Sharon Harris, *A Little Giant Book: Science Facts* (Sterling, 2007), 138.

During World War II, Congress officially changed the name of sauerkraut to "liberty cabbage." *To retaliate, the Germans—and the rest of the world—continued to not eat American cheese.*

> Leland Gregory, *Stupid History: Tales of Stupidity, Strangeness, and Mythconceptions Throughout the Ages* (Andrews McMeel, 2007), 36.

As a form of punishment in many American prisons, misbehaving inmates are put on a temporary diet of "prison loaf." The "food" resembles meatloaf and contains a combination of vegetables, wheat bread, artificial cheeses, greens, beans, nuts, berries, and any number of other ingredients. *Today I learned I would eat better in prison.*

> ❯ Scott Simon, "Prison Loaf," NPR, April 6, 2002, *www.npr.org.*

A ban on products containing sheep's lungs means Scottish haggis cannot enter the United States. *Trust me, we aren't missing out on much.*

> ❯ Stephen Mulvey, "U.S. Not Ready to Lift Ban on Scottish Haggis," BBC News, January 2010. *www.bbc.co.uk.*

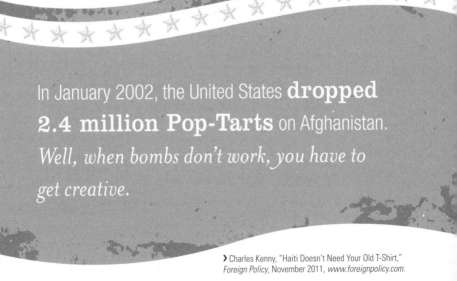

In January 2002, the United States **dropped 2.4 million Pop-Tarts** on Afghanistan. *Well, when bombs don't work, you have to get creative.*

> ❯ Charles Kenny, "Haiti Doesn't Need Your Old T-Shirt," *Foreign Policy*, November 2011, *www.foreignpolicy.com.*

You can create more than 2 million different sandwich combinations at a Subway restaurant. *Unfortunately, they are all still Subway sandwiches.*

❯ "FAQ," Subway, *www.subway.com.*

American breweries produce
6 billion gallons of beer each year.
Which is clearly not enough.

❯ A. P. Holiday, *Hmm . . . I Did Not Know That* (Haymaker Book Company, 2011).

An eight-ounce package of raisins may contain nine or more whole or equivalent insects. *Which means that somewhere out there is a person whose job it is to determine how many random legs equals one whole bug.*

❯ "Food Defect Action Levels," U.S. Food and Drug Administration Center for Food Safety and Applied Nutrition, July 2011, *www.fda.gov.*

Americans throw away 2.5 million plastic bottles every hour. *Would they rather we become a nation of hoarders?*

❯ Jessica Williams, *50 Facts That Should Change the World 2.0* (The Disinformation Company, 2007), 227.

One in four bottles of water sold in the United States is merely bottled tap water. *You can almost taste the tears of joy shed by the manufacturer.*

> Josh Peterson, "Which Is Healthier: Tap Water or Bottled Water?," Planet Green, April 27, 2009, *www.planetgreen.discovery.com*.

Ben & Jerry's was the first name-brand ice cream to be taken into space. *Perfect for when astronauts want to crawl into bed, eat an entire pint alone, and have a good cry.*

> Danielle Coots, "Ben & Jerry's to Curve [sic] Your Ice Cream Craving," Examiner.com, July 26, 2011, *www.examiner.com*.

In 1985, Ben & Jerry's ice cream provided a pig farm in Stowe, Vermont, with leftover ice cream to feed the livestock. According to the farmer, the pigs gladly devoured every flavor except Mint Oreo, which they refused to eat. *Pigs need to spend less time being snobby and more time becoming bacon.*

> Dawn Gibeau, "Ice Cream with a Different Flavor: Ben & Jerry's Offers Taste of Productivity, Social Activism, Fun," *National Catholic Reporter*, May 27, 1994. *www.ncronline.org*.

CHAPTER 5

From the Greenbrier Ghost to the Amityville Horror

Horrifying American Hauntings to Frighten

When it comes to ghosts, people generally fall into one of two camps:

1. Yah, right. I suppose you believe in the tooth fairy too?
2. Oh sure, I believe in ghosts. I have one who lives in my left sock actually. Want to meet him?

Unfortunately, it's not as cut and dried as that.

Finding facts about ghosts is difficult, but they are definitely out there if you look hard enough. Considering the vast catalog of sightings, encounters, and stories told by reputable sources, even the staunchest skeptic has to consider the possibility that there might just be something to this whole afterlife "nonsense."

Aside from being a famous magician, Harry Houdini was also a devoted skeptic who took it upon himself to dress in costume and attend séances to prove they were hoaxes. *"This stuff is bullshit. Everything I do is real magic, though."*

❯ Marley Gibson, Patrick Burns, and Dave Schrader, *The Other Side: A Teen's Guide to Ghost Hunting and the Paranormal* (Graphia, 2009), 4.

Noted hypnotist and parapsychologist Ralph Bibbo has visited the Stone's Public House in Ashland, Massachusetts, on several occasions and determined that the inn is home to at least six ghosts. *"Noted hypnotist" seems oxymoronic.*

❯ Varla Ventura, *Book of the Bizarre: Freaky Facts and Strange Stories* (Red Wheel, 2008), 9–12.

The Los Angeles Pet Memorial Park is home to the remains of Hopalong Cassidy's horse Topper, Petey the dog from "Our Gang," and Humphrey Bogart's cat Boots. Some believe the cemetery is haunted by the ghost of Kabar, Rudolph Valentino's Great Dane. *A live Great Dane will always be more intimidating than a dead one.*

❯ "Surprising Spot for a Holiday Wonderland: Los Angeles Pet Memorial Park in Calabasas," *Los Angeles Times*, December 28, 2009, *www.latimes.com/ news/blogs*.

Visitors to New York's Washington Square have reported a number of ghost sightings over the years. Many attribute this to the fact that the site once played host to public executions. *And people also use a lot of drugs there.*

❯ Joshua Gee, *Encyclopedia Horrifica* (Scholastic, 2007), 75.

When a terrible fire struck the LaLaurie Mansion of New Orleans in 1834, firefighters were shocked to discover a veritable torture chamber in the attic. The mansion's mistress, Delphine LaLaurie, kept several of her slaves chained upstairs where she mutilated their bodies and left them to rot. *Annnnnndddd there's nothing funny about that. At all.*

> Joanna Austin, Mark Moran, and Mark Scuerman, *Weird Hauntings: True Tales of Ghostly Places* (Sterling Publishing, 2006), 85–89.

The Dorrington Hotel in High Sierra, California, is named for Rebecca Dorrington, a woman who suffered a fatal fall down a flight of stairs there in 1870. Some guests have claimed to witness a phantom recreation of Rebecca's last moments. *Anybody else kind of want to see that? No? Good.*

> Varla Ventura, *Book of the Bizarre: Freaky Facts and Strange Stories* (Red Wheel, 2008), 14.

Death estimates for the Waverly Hills Sanatorium in Louisville, Kentucky, are as high as 63,000, and many believe the tortured souls of the dead still roam the halls. *Apparently we really sucked at treating TB.*

> "Halloween: 13 Haunted Travel Destinations," Lowfares.com, October 26, 2009, *www.lowfares.com*.

More than 20 percent of Americans claim they have seen a ghost or have felt the presence of an apparition. *Approximately the same percentage as have experimented with psychedelic drugs. Coincidence? I think not.*

> Sean Alfano, "Poll: Majority Believe in Ghosts," CBS News, February 11, 2009, *www.cbsnews.com*.

Launch Pad 34 at Florida's Kennedy Space Center has been a persistent source of ghost sightings since 1967, when three astronauts lost their lives following a small explosion at the site. *Are they still astronauts if they die before they leave earth?*

❭ Joanna Austin, Mark Moran, and Mark Scuerman, *Weird Hauntings: True Tales of Ghostly Places* (Sterling Publishing, 2006), 100.

Retired in 1967, the HMS *Queen Mary* cruise ship now rests in Long Beach, California, where it has been the site of more than fifty ghost sightings over the years. Aside from phantom crew members and naval officers, visitors have reported spectral cigar smoke allegedly belonging to the ghost of Winston Churchill. *Because it couldn't possibly be local teens sneaking a smoke.*

❭ "History of Ghost Stories," History Channel, *www.history .com.*

Although the United States Department of Commerce does designate some thirty houses in the United States as "haunted houses," this is not government confirmation of the existence of ghosts. *Besides, do we really want the government sanctioning the afterlife?*

❭ Cherlyn Gardner Strong, "The Whaley House: Government 'Authentication' of Ghosts?," *Tucson Citizen*, November 22, 2009, *www.tucsoncitizen.com.*

Bobby Mackey's Music World in Wilder, Kentucky, was once a slaughterhouse and an alleged site of cult activity. Many believe the well in the basement is actually a portal to hell, a fact that the owner encourages with a warning sign that reads, "Management is not held liable for any attacks by its ghosts." *But if somebody else's ghosts attack you, lawyer up.*

❭ "10 Great Haunted Places Across the USA," *USA Today*, January 10, 2011, *www.usa today.com.*

According to reports, if you visit El Paso's Concordia Cemetery just after midnight, you can hear the ghostly sounds of children laughing and playing among the graves. *But only if you bring your own children and encourage them to laugh and play.*

> Brad Steiger, *Real Ghosts, Restless Spirits, and Haunted Places* (Visible Ink Press, 2003), 572.

For $200, you can arrange for an overnight investigation of the Washoe Club's famous haunted crypt and spiral staircase for you and a small group of fellow ghost hunters. *But remember, filming it doesn't make you a ghost hunter. It makes you an idiot.*

> "Ghost Hunts and Paranormal Investigations," The Washoe Club Haunted Museum, *www .thewashoeclub.com.*

More than three-quarters of Americans **believe in life after death**, yet 87 percent feel science will never be able to provide proof that it exists. *Convenient.*

> Sean Alfano, "Poll: Majority Believe in Ghosts," CBS News, February 11, 2009, *www.cbsnews.com.*

Dan Aykroyd's father, Peter Aykroyd, is an actual ghostbuster. He has even written a book about his experiences with the paranormal. *Giving yourself an arbitrary title does not make you that thing.*

❯ J. F. Sargent, "7 Movies That Put Insane Work into Details You Didn't Notice," *Cracked*, November 30, 2011, *www.cracked.com*.

Before he got his break as a musician,

Rod Stewart worked briefly as a grave digger.

Good to know he has something to fall back on.

❯ Varla Ventura, *Book of the Bizarre: Freaky Facts and Strange Stories* (Red Wheel, 2008), 209.

Cars that stop on a section of railroad tracks south of San Antonio are often pushed out of harm's way by what many believe are dozens of tiny ghostly hands belonging to a group of children who were killed when their bus stalled on the same tracks. *How do we know they aren't just trying to push us into oncoming traffic?*

❯ "The 10 Most Haunted Cities in America," CNBC, *www.cnbc.com*.

The Myrtles Plantation in Louisiana is supposedly home to as many as twelve ghosts, the most well known of which is "Chloe," a slave owned by Clark and Sara Woodruff who was allegedly murdered when Sara suspected she had been carrying on an affair with her husband. *I like to think the punishment for people like the Woodruffs is an eternity of being Andre the Giant's bitch.*

❯ "Top 10 Most Haunted Places," Listverse, August 22, 2007, *www.listverse.com*.

While staying in room 217 at the Stanley Hotel in Estes Park, Colorado, author Stephen King's rest was reportedly interrupted when he heard ghost children playing in the hallway. He later used the incident as inspiration for his novel *The Shining. And Redrum was the name of his childhood sled. Or something like that.*

❯ "10 Most Haunted Places On Earth," Environmental Graffiti, *www.environmentalgraffiti.com.*

The Stanley Hotel is so proud of its connection to King's novel that it plays the 1980 Stanley Kubrick film adaptation for its guests on a continuous loop. *Because just staying in a haunted hotel isn't creepy enough on its own.*

❯ Kat Valentine King, "A Good Day to Get Spooked at the Stanley Museum," *The Denver Post*, October 31, 2009, *www.denverpost.com.*

On December 20, 1820, Tennessee resident John Bell may have become the first American killed by a ghost. He drank a bottle of poison allegedly set out for him by the specter Old Kate who had haunted his cabin for years. *I long for the days when you could kill someone and blame it on a ghost.*

❯ Joshua Gee, *Encyclopedia Horrifica* (Scholastic, 2007), 37.

Many believe that the ghost of Junius Brutus Booth, the father of John Wilkes Booth, can be seen walking backstage at the Dock Street Theater in Charleston, South Carolina. *I wonder if he's disappointed or proud. I mean, his son grew up to be an assassin, but at least he was a successful one.*

❯ "Top 10 Most Haunted Cities in the U.S.," TopTenz.net, *www.toptenz.net.*

Shortly after Elva Zona Heaster was found dead in Greenbrier County, West Virginia, her mother claimed she was visited by Elva's ghost. Elva claimed her husband Erasmus Shue had broken her neck and spun her head completely around. Sure enough, when police exhumed the body, the story of the Greenbrier Ghost checked out and Shue was found guilty of the murder. *An open and shut case . . . if you're an idiot.*

❯ Scott McCabe, "Crime History: 'Greenbrier Ghost' Helps Solve Murder," *Washington Examiner*, January 22, 2011, *www.washingtonexaminer.com.*

Many ghost hunters attribute the public interest in ghosts to the Fox sisters, a pair of mediums who toured the country performing séances in the mid-nineteenth century. Their communions with the dead involved knocking noises, levitating tables, and strange sounds allegedly caused by the deceased loved ones of those present. *I'm not going to say they were frauds. I sincerely hope that's not necessary.*

❯ Marley Gibson, Patrick Burns, and Dave Schrader, *The Other Side: A Teen's Guide to Ghost Hunting and the Paranormal* (Graphia, September 14, 2009), 2.

The fear of ghosts is called phasmophobia. *If a fear applies to everyone on earth, it does not need its own special name.*

❯ *National Geographic Kids, Weird But True: 300 Outrageous Facts* (*National Geographic* Children's Books, 2009), 29.

One of the most popular exhibits at the Key West Museum of Art & History is an unassuming doll that goes by the name of Robert. According to various reports, the doll is possessed and has been known to throw furniture and pace around the room from time to time. *I'm pretty sure I could handle a doll. Even a possessed one.*

❯ "Top 10 Most Haunted Cities in the U.S.," TopTenz.net, *www .toptenz.net.*

Thomas Edison developed and tested a device to communicate

with the dead, but there is no evidence that he was ever successful. *If it had worked, we'd be able to ask him.*

> Joshua Gee, *Encyclopedia Horrifica* (Scholastic, 2007), 47.

There have been reports of the ghost of Benjamin Franklin appearing near the library of the American Philosophical Society in Philadelphia since the late nineteenth century. Some witnesses insist his statue comes to life and dances in the streets. *If you already believe in ghosts, dancing statues really isn't a huge mental leap.*

> "History of Ghost Stories," History Channel, *www.history .com*.

After the untimely death of her husband and child, Sarah Winchester was informed by a local seer that her house was haunted, and only unceasing construction on the house would keep the spirits at bay. So Sarah started building—and didn't stop for thirty-eight years. *If you're going to be dead, might as well mess with the living.*

> "Top 10 Haunted Places," *Time*, October 30, 2008, *www.time.com*.

In 1989 Jeffrey Stambovsky purchased the infamous Ackley house in Nyack, New York, not realizing that everyone else in town believed it to be haunted. When the owner refused to buy back the house, Stambovsky took her to court— and won. *Just because you're a judge, that doesn't mean you're not a dumbass.*

❯ Joshua Gee, *Encyclopedia Horrifica* (Scholastic, 2007), 42.

Visitors to the infamous Alcatraz prison in San Francisco have reported hearing spectral banjo music coming from inside Al Capone's old cell. *Learning the banjo was easy. Hiding the tape recorder was the hard part.*

❯ "History of Ghost Stories," History Channel, *www.history .com*.

Americans spend more than **$13 billion** annually on funerals. *Mine will cost whatever money I have saved up at the time. So probably about $15.*

❯ Joshua Gee, *Encyclopedia Horrifica* (Scholastic, 2007), 126.

While Abraham Lincoln is one of the most commonly spotted White House ghosts, the residence is also home to the ghost of Abigail Adams, who is occasionally spotted doing laundry in the East Room. *Next to the ghost of Susan B. Anthony shaking her head.*

❯ "Top 10 Haunted Places," *Time*, October 30, 2008, *www.time.com*.

More than half of Americans would

live in a haunted house if they could live there rent-free.

I'd live inside of a haunted dumpster if it was free.

❯ "USA Today Snapshots," *USA Today, www.usatoday.com*.

The Villisca Ax Murder House was the location of a brutal murder of six children and their parents in 1912. Since then, there have been numerous reports of moving orbs, disembodied whispers, and sightings of ghostly children playing in the halls. Should you wish to judge for yourself, the site is open to overnight visitors. *No thanks. I choose life.*

❯ "Halloween: 13 Haunted Travel Destinations," Lowfares. com, October 26, 2009, *www.lowfares.com*.

Built in 1829, Philadelphia's Eastern State Penitentiary was the first prison to institute solitary confinement, and it is also allegedly one of the most haunted. Aside from the sounds of feet shuffling in empty cells, and moaning wails drifting through dark corridors, Cell Block 12 is famous for an eerie, disembodied laughter that echoes through the prison. *Not sure I'd laugh if I were in solitary confinement for eternity.*

❯ "Top 10 Haunted Places," *Time*, October 30, 2008, *www.time.com*.

Port Tobacco, Maryland, is home to a blood-stained rock known locally as "Peddler's Rock." Residents insist it is home to the Blue Dog, an apparition that guards its dead master's buried treasure. *Not to be confused with the Red Dog, which guards his dead master's shitty beer collection.*

❯ Varla Ventura, *Book of the Bizarre: Freaky Facts and Strange Stories* (Red Wheel, 2008), 19.

Although Chicago's White Lady, an apparition clad in white often spotted carrying a baby through the Bachelor's Grove cemetery, is the most famous ghost in the area, she is certainly not the only peculiarity associated with the location. The site was rumored to be a favorite body dumping ground for Prohibition-era gangsters. Visitors have reported everything from wandering headstones to satanic cults that have taken up residence in the cemetery. *Note to self: Bachelor's Grove is way less awesome than it sounds.*

❯ "Top 10 Most Haunted Cities in the U.S.," TopTenz.net, *www.toptenz.net.*

Thirty-seven percent of Americans believe in the notion of haunted houses.

Only 4 percent less than the number of people who believe in evolution. Jesus tapdancing Christ.

❯ David W. Moore, "Three in Four Americans Believe in Paranormal," Gallup, June 16, 2005, *www.gallup.com.*

In early 2000, an anonymous seller posted the first haunted object on eBay. The painting was titled *The Hands Resist Him* by Bill Stoneham, and the seller alleged that the young boy and girl depicted in the painting came to life at random intervals and moved about the painting. *It's on eBay, so it must be real.*

> "The Ebay Haunted Painting," BBC, July 2002, *www.bbc.co.uk*.

Although a buyer did eventually purchase the haunted painting for $1,050, he has yet to experience anything paranormal. *A fool and his money are soon parted.*

> "The Ebay Haunted Painting," BBC, July 2002, *www.bbc.co.uk*.

Many people consider the Joshua Ward House in Salem, Massachusetts, to be the most haunted house in America. The structure was built on the foundation of the home of George Corwin, the man who served as sheriff during the Salem Witch Trials. *Some people just deserve to be haunted for eternity.*

> "Top 10 Most Haunted Cities in the U.S.," TopTenz.net, *www.toptenz.net*.

If you visit the crypt belonging to Eunice Welsh near Bridgewater, New York, and knock twice, legend has it that the ghost of Eunice will knock back. *Some people say hiding in a crypt to freak out passersby is a waste of my time. Some people are wrong.*

> Mark Moran, Mark Sceurman, and Matt Lake, *Weird U.S. The ODDyssey Continues: Your Travel Guide to America's Local Legends and Best Kept Secrets* (Sterling, 2008), 339.

In 1927, a gas storage tank owned by the Equitable Gas Company exploded, destroying hundreds of homes in the Pittsburgh area. One of the homes destroyed was the Congelier Mansion, a building previously believed to be the most haunted home in America. *Some problems are best solved with explosives.*

> Albrecht Powell, "The Original Most Haunted House in America," About .com, *www.Pittsburgh .about.com.*

Before guests may stay in room 204 at the 1790 Inn in Savannah, Georgia, they must sign a waiver releasing management of all responsibility should any items of clothing be stolen by the hotel's resident ghost "Anne." *Something tells me that "Anne" is a creepy, lonely bellhop with an underwear fetish and lots of free time.*

> Brad Steiger, *Real Ghosts, Restless Spirits, and Haunted Places* (Visible Ink Press, 2003), 577.

Concerned that the set of the 1973 film *The Exorcist* was actually possessed by evil spirits, director William Friedkin asked Reverend Thomas Bermingham to visit the set and give a blessing to reassure the cast and crew. *I find blowtorches are much more effective than holy water.*

> "The Exorcist," IMDb, *www.imdb.com.*

According to William Peter Blatty, the author of *The Exorcist*, he wrote the book to reaffirm the reader's faith in God. He never intended it to be scary.
If by "God" he meant "creepy prepubescent girl spitting out green vomit," then mission accomplished.

> William Peter Blatty, "'The Exorcist's' Secret Message," Fox News, October 28, 2011, *www.foxnews.com.*

Many popular haunted locales play host to large machinery or environmental factors that generate "infrasound," noises below the range of human hearing. These noises can cause everything from pain and nausea to a feeling of dread. *Who are you going to believe, the lunatic in the lab coat or the calm, collected hillbilly speaking in tongues?*

❯ "Infrasound," The Skeptic's Dictionary," *www.skeptic.com.*

More than 80 percent of elderly people experience hallucinations associated with their dead partner one month after bereavement.

You say, "hallucinations," I say, "ghosts." You say, "potato," I say, "primordial French fries."

❯ Vaughan Bell, "Ghost Stories: Visits From the Deceased," *Scientific American*, December 2, 2008, *www.scientific american.com.*

Residents of Reading, Pennsylvania, claim the ghosts of Mrs. Bissinger and her children haunt the area near the Union Lock Canal where the family drowned in 1875. Visitors report feeling an overwhelming sad and horrific energy when they visit the spot. *You'd be sad too if you were trapped in Reading, Pennsylvania, for eternity.*

❯ Varla Ventura, *Book of the Bizarre: Freaky Facts and Strange Stories* (Red Wheel, 2008), 20.

When his daughter complained of hearing ghostly rapping noises in the middle of the night, President Harry S. Truman attributed it to a dangerous settling of the floors. As it turned out, the building was in imminent danger of collapse, and some believe the rapping sounds were the ghost of Abraham Lincoln trying to warn the family. *Because it couldn't have actually been the floors settling or anything.*

> "Famous Ghosts in American History," History Channel, *www.history.com.*

When Woodrow Wilson's second wife ordered workers to dig up former First Lady "Dolley" Dorothy Madison's beloved rose garden, **the ghost of Dolley appeared** and berated the workers for threatening her garden. They promptly fled, and the garden still remains today. *Rule Number 1: don't mess with dead people's stuff.*

> "Famous Ghosts in American History," History Channel, *www.history.com.*

Boston's Majestic Theater is said to be one of the most haunted theaters in the city. Many patrons have reported the ghost of one of Boston's former mayors sitting in the very seat in which he died. *That's actually just the current mayor. He doesn't do much . . .*

> Brad Steiger, *Real Ghosts, Restless Spirits, and Haunted Places* (Visible Ink Press, 2003), 571.

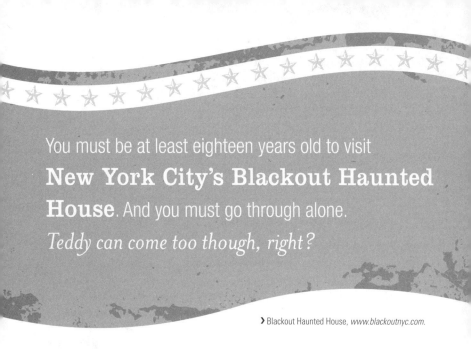

You must be at least eighteen years old to visit **New York City's Blackout Haunted House**. And you must go through alone. *Teddy can come too though, right?*

> Blackout Haunted House, *www.blackoutnyc.com.*

On a cold December evening in 1955, Commander Brougham aboard the USS *Constellation* snapped a picture of a "phosphorescently glowing, translucent ectoplasmic manifestation of a late eighteenth-century or early nineteenth-century sailor, complete with gold stripe trousers, cocked hat, and sword." *When in doubt, just shove a bunch of scientific-sounding words together and hope for the best.*

> "Famous Ghosts in American History," History Channel, *www.history.com.*

In 1964 a priest arrived on board the USS *Constellation* to find there was nobody there to greet him. Luckily when he wandered below deck he found a knowledgeable old sailor who showed him around. When he went above deck he encountered several of the regular tour guides who informed him there were no men below. *So ghosts are real and make excellent tour guides.*

> "Famous Ghosts in American History," History Channel, *www.history.com.*

During the 1800s, prisoners at Philadelphia's Eastern State Penitentiary were locked alone in their cells twenty-four hours a day, with the exception of two thirty-minute exercise periods. The building is now open to the public, and many claim they can still hear the anguished moans of the lonely prisoners. *That's just the groans of 100 collective children forced to visit a prison instead of going to Disney World.*

❯ Jan Payne, *The World's Best Book: The Spookiest, Smelliest, Wildest, Oldest, Weirdest, Brainiest, and Funniest Facts* (Running Press Kids, 2009).

Many American theaters are closed on Mondays to allow the ghosts that haunt them an opportunity to put on their own plays. *The acting is never any good, but the production values are spectacular.*

❯ Varla Ventura, *Beyond Bizarre: Frightening Facts and Blood-Curdling True Tales* (Weiser Books, 2010), 55.

A headless ghost is said to patrol San Francisco's Bay Bridge where he knocks on the windows of passing motorists. Many believe he was a victim of the 1989 earthquake. *The homeless in San Francisco are really dedicated to their craft.*

❯ Brad Steiger, *Real Ghosts, Restless Spirits, and Haunted Places* (Visible Ink Press, 2003), 577.

Visitors to New York City's White Horse Tavern may encounter the ghost of poet Dylan Thomas, who drank a fatal eighteen shots of scotch there in 1953. According to witnesses, he still prefers his usual corner table. *There are worse ways to go.*

❯ "History of Ghost Stories," History Channel, *www.history .com*.

Although the building that played host to the infamous 1929 Valentine's Day Massacre—in which seven of Bugs Moran's men were executed by members of Al Capone's gang—has been demolished, many witnesses claim to have seen shadowy spirits wandering around the area and to have heard the sound of machine-gun fire. *There's nothing strange about seeing shady people and hearing gunshots in Chicago.*

❯ Brad Steiger, *Real Ghosts, Restless Spirits, and Haunted Places* (Visible Ink Press, 2003), 572.

After purchasing the "Amityville Horror House" for $80,000 in 1975, the Lutz family fled just twenty-eight days later, citing a host of supernatural events such as slime oozing down walls, strange odors, moving furniture, swarms of flies in the dead of winter, and slamming doors. *For $80,000, deal with it.*

❯ Diane Tuman, "Top 10 Haunted Homes In the U.S.," MSNBC, October 25, 2010, *www.msnbc.msn.com.*

The Lutz family later admitted that their claims of supernatural phenomena were all an elaborate hoax. *<golf clap>*

❯ Diane Tuman, "Top 10 Haunted Homes In the U.S.," MSNBC, October 25, 2010, *www.msnbc.msn.com.*

Although park officials deny the claims, reports abound that visitors to Disney World routinely scatter the ashes of deceased loved ones in the park's Haunted Mansion ride. Some visitors claim that the result of one such impromptu ceremony is the ghost of a seven-year-old boy often spotted crying at the ride's exit. *This sends a terrible message to the nation's youth. "If you die young, you can go on the rides forever!"*

❯ Jeff Baham, "Human Ashes Scattered at Walt Disney World Haunted Mansion, Again," *The Examiner*, May 17, 2009, *www.examiner.com.*

Many claim the ghosts of dead soldiers still wander the field

of Gettysburg searching for their missing rifles and fallen comrades. *To be fair, there are plenty of living Americans who don't realize the Civil War is over.*

❯ "Top 10 Haunted Places," *Time*, October 30, 2008, *www.time.com*.

In 2002, The American Institute of Parapsychology named Savannah, Georgia, as America's most haunted city. *Too bad the AIP is about as reputable as that kid in middle school who insisted you could "catch gay" from a toilet seat.*

❯ "10 Most Haunted Cities in America," *The Huffington Post*, September 30, 2010, *www.huffingtonpost.com*.

Numerous motorists traveling on Archer Avenue in Chicago have reported the apparition of a young female hitchhiker wearing a white party dress. The young woman appears normal until she asks to be let out at the Resurrection Cemetery, steps out of the car, and vanishes into thin air. *Which is why you should always pinch hitchhikers before you agree to let them ride in your car.*

❯ "The 10 Most Haunted Cities in America," CNBC, *www.cnbc.com*.

CHAPTER 8

Only Twenty Miles to Creepy Giant Puppets!

Strange Roadside Attractions Across the United States to Visit

If there's one thing we Americans love, it's being bigger and better than the rest of the world. Which might explain why there is a four-way dispute over which town is home to the world's largest ball of twine or why there's an archway in Wyoming made from 3,000 elk antlers.

While it's true that some of these strange roadside attractions may seem odd and slightly cringeworthy, each and every one of them is interesting in its own right. And while they may not all be worth going out of your way to see, they are certainly worth reading about.

Despite not owning any stake in the properties, early twentieth-century con man George C. Parker successfully sold the Brooklyn Bridge, the Statue of Liberty, the Metropolitan Museum of Art, and Grant's Tomb to various individuals on more than one occasion. *"But he gave me the 'nice face' discount. How could I pass that up?"*

❯ Gabriel Cohen, "For You, Half Price," *The New York Times*, November 27, 2005, *www.nytimes.com*.

Believing that the soul exited the body during one's dying breath, Henry Ford captured the final gasp of his dear friend Thomas Edison in a test tube. The morbid artifact is now on display at Henry Ford's Museum in Dearborn, Michigan. *"I'll miss you buddy. Is it cool if I trap your eternal soul in Dearborn, Michigan, for all eternity?"*

❯ "Thomas Edison's Last Breath," *Roadside America*, *www.roadsideamerica.com*.

Until it was chopped down by vandals in late 2010, the aptly named "Shoe Tree," a cottonwood adorned with hundreds upon hundreds of sneakers, loafers, boots, and every other form of footwear imaginable, stood on Highway 50 in Nevada. *According to my limited knowledge of urban culture, you could also buy drugs there.*

❯ Nevada's Landmark 'Shoe Tree' Cut Down, United Press International, January 4, 2011, *www.upi.com*.

There have been four versions of the "World's Largest Egg" throughout the history of Winlock, Washington, where it's displayed. The current version is made of fiberglass and weighs 1,200 pounds. *A word of advice, Winlock: If somebody builds a bigger one, just let it go.*

❯ Val Bromann, "15 of the Weirdest Roadside Attractions in America," *BootsnAll*, May 24, 2011, *www.bootsnall.com*.

If you can't be bothered to head out to the real Graceland in Memphis, you can always settle for Roanoke, Virginia's miniature version. The hand-crafted structures at Miniature Graceland include the mansion itself, a replica of the Elvis Presley Car Museum, as well as the city of Tupelo (the King's birthplace). *And no, Elvis did not use a shrinking machine to miniaturize himself and fade into obscurity in Mini Graceland. He's dead.*

❯ Tad Dickens, "Burnin' Love: Local Musicians Take On Restoration of Miniature Graceland," *The Roanoke Times*, August 23, 2011, *www.roanoke.com*.

While you might think an art installation consisting of ten vintage Cadillacs sitting upright, half-buried in the dirt is weird enough, you'd be wrong. Visitors to the Cadillac Ranch off of Route 66 in Amarillo, Texas, are also encouraged to spray paint graffiti on the cars, which are repainted every so often. *And yes, it's full of drawings of penises. Naturally.*

❯ Val Bromann, "15 of the Weirdest Roadside Attractions in America," *BootsnAll*, May 24, 2011, *www.bootsnall.com*.

Wall Drug, a drug store in Wall, South Dakota sporting an 80-foot-tall plastic brontosaurus, originally rose in popularity in the 1930s for offering free water to wayward travelers. *"Come for the free water; stay because there's literally nowhere else to go."*

❯ Nancy Prichard Bouchard, "The Top Ten U.S. Roadside Attractions," Away.com, *www.away.com*.

Every time Wander Martich of Grand Rapids, Michigan, received a paycheck, she put $20 worth of pennies into a jar. About 84,000 pennies later, Martrich decided to put her coinage to good use and created a ten-foot-tall sculpture made entirely of pennies. The subject of her work of art? A penny, of course. *Anybody else feel 84,000 of anything should be worth more than $840?*

❯ Dan Philibin, "Abe Would Be Amazed at Giant Penny Sculpture," Ripley's Believe It or Not!," February 7, 2011, *www.ripleys.com.*

Seattle's Ye Olde Curiosity Shop contained such a large collection of mummified remains, two-headed animals, shrunken heads, and other oddities that they had to open up a Ye Olde Curiosity Shop Too just a stone's throw away. *Awesome. Two places to avoid like the plague for the price of one.*

❯ Matt Lake and Randy Fairbanks, *Weird U.S.: A Freaky Field Trip Through the 50 States* (Sterling, 2011), 7.

Bronner's Christmas Wonderland in Frankenmuth, Michigan, is the self-proclaimed world's largest Christmas store. The amount of electricity required to run the 100,000 lights that illuminate the sales floor costs approximately $1,250 per day. *Because nothing says "Christmas" like wasting enormous sums of cash.*

❯ "Merchandise and Display Information," Bronner's Christmas Wonderland, *www.bronners.com.*

The World's Largest Buffalo, in Jamestown, North Dakota—a sixty-ton structure built to lure drivers into town off the interstate—remained nameless for more than fifty years until it was dubbed "Dakota Thunder" following a 2010 naming contest. *Bonus fact: "Buffalo buffalo Buffalo buffalo buffalo buffalo Buffalo buffalo." is a grammatically correct sentence.*

❯ Val Bromann, "15 of the Weirdest Roadside Attractions in America," *BootsnAll*, May 24, 2011, *www.bootsnall.com.*

If you ever wondered what would happen if giant dinosaurs had fought during the Civil War, you need look no further than Natural Bridge, Virginia's Dinosaur Kingdom. Visitors to the quirky destination are treated to scores of giant plastic lizards devouring Union soldiers in various "re-enactments" of famous battles. *If you are going to rewrite history, might as well go for broke.*

> John Fiuffo, "Weird Roadside Attractions," *Forbes*, November 23, 2010, *www.Forbes.com.*

If visitors to Dinosaur Kingdom get bored of prehistoric carnage, they can join the nearby **"Hunt Bigfoot with a Redneck"** tour, where guests join guide J. P. Innerbred to search for the elusive creature who stole his prized Big Mouth Billy wall fixture. *I wish I made that one up. I really do.*

> "Hunt Bigfoot with a Redneck," *Flashnews*, July 20, 2010, *www.flashnews.com.*

Although often overshadowed by the original Mount Rushmore in South Dakota, Missouri's Mount Rushmore with Fake Celebrity Heads can still attract a crowd. The monument depicts John Wayne, Elvis, Marilyn Monroe, and Oliver Hardy. *Both attractions are equally dumb, but for different reasons.*

> "Mount Rushmore with Fake Celebrity Heads," *Roadside America*, *www.roadsideamerica.com.*

The world's largest bull is Albert, a forty-five-ton concrete statue in Audubon, Iowa, named after local banker Albert Kruse in the 1960s. He stands thirty feet tall and possesses an internal steel frame constructed from dismantled windmills. *Down with green energy, up with novelty statues!*

❯ "12 Strange Tourist Attractions," How Stuff Works, *www.tlc.howstuffworks.com.*

When patrons of the Maid Rite Sandwich Shop in Greenville, Ohio, polish off one of the store's signature sandwiches, they show their appreciation in the traditional way—by sticking a piece of gum on the building's exterior. The practice started in the 1950s, and now tourists come from far and wide to view the collage of gum that adorns the brick exterior. *Come on people, it's literally garbage stuck to a wall.*

❯ Brian Butko, *Roadside Attractions: Cool Cafes, Souvenir Stands, Route 66 Relics, & Other Road Trip Fun* (Stackpole Books, 2007), 142.

From 1882 to 1899, the U.S. Patent Office granted James Lafferty exclusive rights to build animal-shaped buildings. He used this temporary monopoly to construct "Lucy," a sixty-foot-long, ninety-ton wooden elephant in Margate, New Jersey. Lucy still stands to this day, making it the oldest known zoomorphic architectural building. *Cool?*

❯ "Top 10 Must-See Roadside Attractions," TopTenz.net, *www.toptenz.net.*

One of the largest hockey sticks in the world can be found in Eveleth, Minnesota. The stick is 107 feet long and is accompanied by a 700-pound puck. *Dontcha know.*

> ❯ "World's Strangest Tourist Attractions," *Open Travel*, May 31, 2010, *www.opentravel.com.*

To celebrate the discovery of vast oil reserves in the area, in 1953 the city of Tulsa, Oklahoma, erected a twenty-two-ton concrete and iron statue of a golden man standing next to an oil derrick. The Golden Driller is seventy-six feet tall and can withstand a 200 mph tornado. *But can he withstand the Green Movement?*

> ❯ Kayla Webley, "Top 50 American Roadside Attractions: Golden Driller, Tulsa, Okla.," *Time*, July 28, 2010, *www.time.com.*

In 1979 the Golden Driller was declared Oklahoma's official state monument. A plaque at its base reads, "To the men of the petroleum industry who by their vision and daring have created from God's abundance a better life for mankind." *It sounds silly, but there was literally nothing better to choose from.*

> ❯ Kayla Webley, "Top 50 American Roadside Attractions: Golden Driller, Tulsa, Okla.," *Time*, July 28, 2010, *www.time.com.*

From 1950 to 1967, citizens of Fort Bragg, California, unceremoniously dumped tons of garbage onto the nearby beach. Over the decades, the ocean transformed the refuse into thousands of small, smooth glass pebbles that litter the shoreline today. Now known as Glass Beach, the area attracts thousands of treasure seekers every year. *Dumb people love shiny things.*

> ❯ Christopher Reynolds, "The Fetid Underbelly of Glass Beach," *Los Angeles Times*, August 3, 2004, *www.latimes.com.*

Although the rural town of Metropolis, Illinois, is a far cry from the bustling imaginary city featured in the *Superman* comics, the town has embraced their superhero ties and proudly declare themselves as the "Hometown of Superman." A fifteen-foot bronze statue of the Man of Steel sits on Main Street. *For the love of Odin, Superman's "hometown" was actually the planet Krypton. And his name is Kal-El. And did I mention I'm single?*

> ❯ "12 Strange Tourist Attractions," How Stuff Works, *www.tlc.howstuffworks.com.*

One hundred miles east of Denver in Genoa, Colorado, sits the Wonder Tower, a tribute to all things weird and obscure. The sixty-five-foot tower is home to stuffed two-headed animals, a collection of 50,000 glass bottles, rooster eyeglasses, and scores of other curiosities. If guests climb to the top, they can allegedly view six different states. *Genoa, Colorado: a place you'd pay not to visit.*

> ❯ Nancy Prichard Bouchard, "The Top Ten U.S. Roadside Attractions," Away.com, *www.away.com.*

About 150 miles southeast of El Paso, Texas, sits the Marfa Prada Store. Although the doors are permanently locked, you can view all of the high-end wares through the window without ever having to go inside. The store only contains twenty left-foot shoes and six purses. *Good to know that not even Texas is immune to the smug epidemic plaguing the country.*

❯ "America's Strangest Roadside Attractions," *Travel and Leisure,* www.travelandleisure.com.

In 1977 Mike Carmichael of Alexandria, Indiana, applied

a single coat of paint to a regulation baseball. He has repeated the process every day since then, and after more than 17,000 coats his nine-inch ball has ballooned to more than 104 inches, weighing 1,100 pounds. *I imagine he wishes he'd just played catch.*

❯ Dan Philibin, "Now This Is Paintball," Ripley's Believe It or Not!, July 25, 2011, *www.ripleys.com.*

In honor of High Point, North Carolina's status as the "Home Furnishings Capital of the World," the city erected the world's largest chest of drawers in 1926. Originally known as the "Bureau of Information," the structure stands thirty-eight feet high. *I wouldn't say you are dumber for knowing that . . . but you certainly aren't smarter.*

❯ Eric Peterson, "8 of the World's Biggest Roadside Attractions," How Stuff Works, *www.tlc.howstuffworks.com.*

While you may think a sixty-eight-foot by twenty-four-foot horseshoe crab seems odd sitting outside of the Freedom Worship Baptist Church in Blanchester, Ohio, the church thinks it is the perfect mascot. Since the horseshoe crab has changed little in 570 million years, church elders feel it makes an excellent case for creationism. *And remember, kids, dinosaur bones were planted as tricks by the Devil. Unless of course it turns out they weren't, in which case it's God's plan.*

❯ "America's Strangest Roadside Attractions," *Travel and Leisure, www.travelandleisure.com.*

The world's largest pistachio nut is thirty feet tall and sits outside McGinn's Pistachio Tree Ranch in Alamogordo, New Mexico. The structure required thirty-five gallons of paint to achieve its signature neon green glow. *I'm starting to doubt that there is an object too mundane to build the world's largest version of it.*

❯ "America's Strangest Roadside Attractions," *Travel and Leisure, www.travelandleisure.com.*

In 2011, Bangerter Homes in Salt Lake City, Utah, constructed an exact replica of the colorful building featured in Disney/Pixar's hit film *Up*. Visitors can pay $10 to tour its interior until the company finds somebody willing to pay the $400,000 price tag to move in. *If it doesn't fly, no thanks.*

❯ Brooks Barnes, "Disney Allows Reproduction of 'Up' House in Utah," *The Seattle Times,* August 26, 2011, *www.seattletimes.com.*

Afton, Wyoming, is home to the world's largest archway constructed out of elk antlers. The elkhorn arch spans Highway 89 and consists of 3,000 elk antlers. *If you listen close, you can actually hear God crying.*

❯ "Afton, Wyoming—World's Largets Elkhorn Arch," *Roadside America, www.roadsideamerica.com.*

Completed in 1977, the Lightning Field is a series of 400 stainless steel poles arranged in a grid in Catron County, New Mexico. The structure can only be viewed by advanced appointment on the condition that visitors agree to spend a full twenty-four hours admiring it. *If you make it exclusive enough, the sheeple will come.*

❯ Todd Gibson, "A Pilgrimage to the Lightning Field," From the Floor, July 25, 2004, *www.fromthefloor.blogspot.com.*

More than 140 feet below the surface of Sweetwater, Tennessee, sits one of the world's largest underground lakes. Visitors can tour the Lost Seas through a system of underground caverns that sport 20,000-year-old jaguar tracks and rare cave formations. *Just beware of the Kraken.*

❯ Ruchika Tulshyan, "Top 50 American Roadside Attractions: The Lost Sea; Sweetwater, TN," *Time*, July 28, 2010, *www.time.com.*

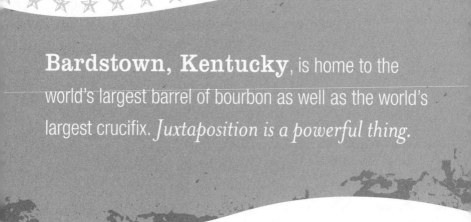

Bardstown, Kentucky, is home to the world's largest barrel of bourbon as well as the world's largest crucifix. *Juxtaposition is a powerful thing.*

❯ "World's Largest Bourbon Barrel," *Roadside America*, www.roadsideamerica.com.

Route 46 near Fargo, North Dakota, features the country's longest straight-away. Drivers can go for 110 miles without having to adjust the steering wheel. *Keep it at a steady 88 mph and we all know what happens.*

> Sheila De La Rosa, *The Encyclopedia of Weird* (Turkids, 2005), 44.

The twenty-foot roadrunner statue that stands sentinel in Las Cruces, New Mexico, may seem odd, but get close and you will discover it's even stranger than you thought—the sculpture is made entirely of garbage. The sculptors salvaged old sneakers, hubcaps, empty bottles, etc. from the local dump to create their giant masterpiece. *May I suggest you don't bother getting closer?*

> "National Border Patrol Museum," *Roadside America*, www.roadsideamerica.com.

The world's largest pipe organ resides in the City Convention Hall in Atlantic City, New Jersey. The massive instrument has seven keyboards, 1,439 stop keys, more than 30,000 pipes, and is capable of producing a sound six times louder than a train whistle. *Much like you, I have no knowledge of ordinary pipe organs, and thus have no idea how impressive this is.*

> Jan Payne, *The World's Best Book: The Spookiest, Smelliest, Wildest, Oldest, Weirdest, Brainiest, and Funniest Facts* (Running Press Kids, 2009).

When weary travelers reach Point Harbor, North Carolina, they can pull off Route 158 and take a rest in the world's largest hammock. The forty-two-foot-long behemoth consists of 10,000 feet of rope and can support upwards of 8,000 pounds. *Nothing more relaxing than taking a nap with your forty-nine closest friends.*

> Amanda Greene, "15 Must-See Roadside Attractions," *Woman's Day*, August 17, 2010, www.womansday.com.

At the Santa's Land store in Cherokee, North Carolina, every day is Christmas. Guests can watch Santa's elves wrapping gifts at Santa's village or head over to Jingle Bell Theater for a magic show. They can even pet Santa's reindeer at the attached zoo. *Nothing says Christmas cheer like penned-up animals.*

❯ Thadra Petkus, "Top 10 Tacky Tourist Sites," Catalogs.com, *www.catalogs.com.*

Niles, Illinois, is home to the Leaning Tower of Niles, a half-scale replica of the Leaning Tower of Pisa. The two tourist locales cemented their bond in 1991 when they became official sister cities. *Only in America would we replicate a failure.*

❯ "America's Strangest Roadside Attractions," *Travel and Leisure, www.travelandleisure.com.*

The Four Corners is the only place in the United States where a person can literally be in four places at once. The location marks the convergence of the borders of Arizona, New Mexico, Utah, and Colorado and costs $3 to visit. *Pro Tip: Save your money and just lie if anybody asks if you went.*

❯ "Four Corners Monument," Utah.com, *www.utah.com.*

While it's true that Middle America is littered with statues of Paul Bunyan, Bemidji, Minnesota, claims to be the first. The town erected their eighteen-foot-tall, two-and-a-half-ton shrine in 1937 and added Bunyan's mythical blue ox, Babe, two years later. *Quite the small victory for Minnesota, but a victory nonetheless.*

❯ Kayla Webley, " Top 50 American Roadside Attractions: Paul Bunyan Statue, Bemidji, MN," *Time*, July 28, 2010, *www.time.com.*

If customers should happen to drop a cocktail glass at Las Vegas's minus5° bar, it's unlikely the bartender would even bat an eye. That's because every-thing, from the bar stools and glasses to the walls, is made of ice. *Save the money and just visit Canada in February.*

❯ "About," minus5° Ice Bar, *www.minus5experience.com.*

Should aliens ever visit Earth, their first stop may very well be Green Bay, Wisconsin. That's because local weld-ing shop owner Bob Tohak built them a landing pad out of an empty fuel tank and scrap iron he had sitting around the shop. The forty-two-foot-tall structure sits on top of his shop on Highway 29 along with a sign that reads: "If the government has no knowledge of aliens why did they make it illegal for U.S. citizens to have any contact with extraterrestrials or their vehicles?" *See the earlier chapter on silly laws where I address this issue.*

❯ "America's Strangest Roadside Attractions," *Travel and Leisure, www.travelandleisure.com.*

Murphy, North Carolina, is home to what may very well be the largest depiction of the Ten Commandments on Earth. Built by the Church of God of Prophecy in 1940, the structure occupies an entire hillside in the Fields of the Wood bible-themed amusement park. *See, Bible thumpers can have fun too. Just as long as it's not actually fun.*

❯ "America's Strangest Roadside Attractions," *Travel and Leisure*, www.travelandleisure.com.

In 1953, a team of philatelists (stamp collectors) at the Boys Town Stamp Collecting Club in Nebraska started construction on a small ball of stamps. Several decades and more than 4,655,000 stamps later, the ball weighs 600 pounds and has a diameter of thirty-two inches. *So sad. So very, very sad.*

❯ Amanda Greene, "15 Must-See Roadside Attractions," *Woman's Day*, August 17, 2010, www.womansday.com.

The Centennial Bulb in Livermore,

California, was turned on for the first time in 1901. It has illuminated the town's firehouse ever since and has only been turned off on two occasions. *Spoiler alert: It's just a bloody light bulb.*

❯ "Facts," Centennial Light, www.centennialbulb.org.

Colorado is home to the town of Dinosaur, a small place where many of the streets carry dinosaur-themed names like Brontosaurus Boulevard and Allosaurus Lane. *Somebody call Jeff Goldblum; there's a town that needs savin'.*

> Google Maps, *www.maps .google.com.*

Cavendish, Vermont, is home to a grotesque monument depicting an iron rod puncturing a human skull. The unique structure was built to honor Phineas Gage, a construction worker who survived having a three-and-a-half-foot rod shot into his skull in 1848. *Sure, he couldn't count to ten afterward, but the knowledge that he was immortal must have been comforting.*

> Bridget Gleeson, "America's Strangest Monuments," AOL Travel, November 10, 2009, *www.travel.aol.com.*

Each year local artists construct murals out of corn to adorn the walls of the Mitchell Corn Palace in Mitchell, South Dakota. After the annual fall harvest, the town allows pigeons and squirrels into the structure to devour the murals and make room for next year's entries. *The best part? Watching the artists watching their work being devoured, of course.*

> "12 Strange Tourist Attractions," How Stuff Works, *www.tlc.howstuffworks.com.*

Thanks to over-farming in the late eighteenth century, Freeport, Maine, is now home to a fifty-acre miniature desert. Visitors can explore the wasteland on foot or take a thirty-minute coach tour. *The rest of the state is not a true desert, just a cultural one.*

> Ruchika Tulshyan, "Desert of Maine, Freeport, Maine, Top 50 American Roadside Attractions," *Time,* July 28, 2010, *www .time.com.*

Visitors to the Mystery Hole in Ansted, West Virginia, are treated to various gravity-defying wonders such as water that flows upward and chairs that support the sitter on just two legs. While most attribute the strange effects to clever architecture, there are some who believe there is some supernatural phenomenon at work that causes the apparent shift in gravity. *The technical term for such people is "asshat."*

> "What is the Mystery Hole?" Mystery Hole, *www.mysteryhole.com*

After visiting a cafe shaped like a coffee pot in the early 1930s, Martin Maurer, a Long Island purveyor of ducks and duck eggs, was inspired to design a similar building for his side business—a twenty-foot-tall building shaped like a duck. The structure still stands today, although patrons can only purchase souvenirs and not ducks and duck eggs. *Takes the guesswork out of shopping.*

> Brian Butko and Sarah Butko, *Roadside Giants* (Stackpole Books, 2005), 9.

If you've ever lost your luggage while flying, chances are it wound up at the Unclaimed Baggage Center in Scottsboro, Alabama. Owner Bryan Owens displays some 7,000 "new" items in his store each day that he purchases from airlines. *There is a special place in hell for that man.*

> Bill Geist, *Way Off the Road* (Broadway Books, 2007), 48–49.

A life-sized watermelon statue sits in the town of Lincoln, Illinois, to commemorate the day that Abraham Lincoln—while eating a watermelon—agreed to let the town carry his name. *They had more obscure options to honor the event, but not many.*

❯ Bridget Gleeson, "America's Strangest Monuments," AOL Travel, November 10, 2009, *www.travel.aol.com.*

The Crazy Horse memorial in South Dakota that honors the Native American leader of the same name is one of the longest construction projects in American history. Sculptor Korczak Ziolkowski started work on the memorial in 1948, and as of 2011 it is still not completed. *We're really good at promising the Native Americans we will do things and then forgetting about them.*

❯ "12 Strange Tourist Attractions," How Stuff Works, *www.tlc.howstuffworks.com.*

In 1996 a reclusive Chinese businessman sought to bring a piece of his homeland to Katy, Texas, in the form of 1:3-scale model of the tomb of Qin Shi Huangdi—complete with 6,000 terra-cotta statues to guard it. The attraction was closed down in 2011 and all of the statues were sold to private collectors. *They make great ash trays.*

❯ Ángel González, "Chinese Takeout: Texans Buy Up Katy's 'Forbidden' Treasures," *Wall Street Journal*, February 22, 2011, *www.wsj.com.*

The world's largest ball of twine constructed by a single person resides in Darwin, Minnesota, and was assembled by Francis A. Johnson from 1950 through 1989. The ball measures thirteen feet in diameter and weighs more than 17,000 pounds. *Thirty-nine years well spent.*

❯ "World's Largest Twine Ball," *Roadside America, www.road sideamerica.com.*

During the 1976 presidential campaign, members of the Indiana Democratic Party constructed a thirteen-foot-tall peanut statue to honor Jimmy Carter's humble beginnings as a peanut farmer. The structure resembles a massive peanut, but sports a toothy grin reminiscent of the former president's. It now resides in Carter's hometown of Plains, Georgia. *Translation: They built a creepy peanut statue and pretended it looked like a president.*

❯ Nate Rawlings, "Top 50 American Roadside Attractions: Jimmy Carter Peanut Statue, Plains, GA," *Time*, July 28, 2010, *www.time.com.*

The world's largest catsup bottle (catsup, not ketchup) is actually a water tower in Collinsville, Illinois, that was designed to look like a bottle of the ubiquitous condiment. The seventy-foot-tall tower was erected in 1949 and still stands today. *Well, you can't just tear down something that beautiful.*

❯ Val Bromann, "15 of the Weirdest Roadside Attractions in America," *BootsnAll*, May 24, 2011, *www.bootsnall.com.*

While the exterior of Massachusetts State Prison inmate James Allen's published deathbed confession may look quite ordinary, it is anything but. The book is bound using some of Allen's own skin. The creepy tome now resides at the Boston Athenæum's Library. *What do you think they used to bind the book you're holding?*

❯ "Narrative of the Life of James Allen, The Highway Man," Boston Athenaeum, *www.bostonathenaeum.org.*

When George Gottbreht of Dunseith, North Dakota, found himself in possession of 2,000 old wheel rims, he did the only logical thing with them—built an eighteen-foot-tall turtle. The Wee'l Turtle pays homage to the nearby Turtle Mountain State Park. *Why recycle when you can build useless crap?*

> ❯ "America's Strangest Roadside Attractions," *Travel and Leisure*, www.travelandleisure.com.

Lenny the Chocolate Moose spends his days in the Len Libby candy shop in Scarborough, Maine. Made from 1,700 pounds of milk chocolate, Lenny was constructed over a one-month period. *You're imagining how much you could eat before somebody realized what was happening. Aren't you?*

> ❯ "America's Strangest Roadside Attractions," *Travel and Leisure*, www.travelandleisure.com.

CHAPTER 7

Be Sure to See Miss Hattie's Bordello Museum!
Odd Museums and Galleries to Seek Out

If you want to know how weird the citizens of a particular country are, you can gauge it by the strange things they do. But a far more accurate measure is to gauge it by what they collect. Judging from some of the museums in this chapter, Americans are about a 9.9 on the Richter Scale of Oddness.

There are things in this chapter that should really never be seen by anyone, let alone an entire second-grade class on a field trip. Yet, for some reason, Americans travel in droves to see everything from Grover Cleveland's tumor to a jacket made entirely of mouse stem cells.

While you may not be able to travel to every museum in this chapter to see such grotesque exhibits for yourself, you can at least get a taste of all the sick, twisted things you are missing out on.

Before his death in 2007, singer Robert Goulet possessed more than 3,000 frog-related trinkets, many of which he purchased from the Museum of Fake Frogs in Eureka Springs, Arkansas. *"Gooooouuullllleeeet." Go Google "Goulet" and "SNL." You'll get it, but I can't promise you'll think it was worth the effort.*

❭ "Frog Fantasies—Museum of Fake Frogs," *Roadside America,* www.roadsideamerica.com.

The rarest, and most valuable, piece on display at the Burlingame, California, Museum of Pez Memorabilia is the "Make a Face" Pez dispenser from the 1970s. Fears children could choke on the removable parts prompted its withdrawal shortly after release. *We really need to stop interfering with Darwinism.*

❭ "Museum of Pez Memorabilia," *Roadside America,* www.roadsideamerica.com.

The most popular exhibit at the National Border Patrol museum in El Paso, Texas, is its section of confiscated items, which contains everything from track-obscuring sandals to homemade motorcycles constructed from old lawnmowers. *God bless those gun-toting rednecks.*

❭ "National Border Patrol Museum," *Roadside America,* www.roadsideamerica.com.

The Edventure Children's Museum in Columbia, South Carolina, is home to "Eddie," a forty-foot, seventeen-and-a-half-ton interactive sculpture of a ten-year-old boy. Visitors to the museum are encouraged to crawl through Eddie's heart, bounce around inside his stomach, and slide out his intestines, to learn more about the inner workings of their bodies. *AKA, pedophile heaven.*

❭ John Fiuffo, "Weird Roadside Attractions," *Forbes,* November 23, 2010, www.Forbes.com.

During the 1992 Los Angeles riots in the wake of the Rodney King beating, several celebrity undergarments were stolen from the Frederick's of Hollywood Lingerie Museum. They included a bustier that had once belonged to Madonna. The singer graciously donated a replacement black corset. *Always thinking of others.*

❯ "Negligees of Note," Roadtrip America, *www.roadtripamerica.com.*

San Francisco's Antique Vibrator Museum follows the history of the vibrator from its humble beginnings as a medical tool used to cure female "hysteria," to its current function as a sexual stimulator. *An orgasm won't cure a woman's hysterics, but it's not a bad place to start.*

❯ Jami Frater, *The Ultimate Book of Top Ten Lists: A Mind-Boggling Collection of Fun, Fascinating and Bizarre Facts on Movies, Music, Sports, Crime, Celebrities, History, Trivia and More* (Ulysses Press, 2009), 23.

The New Hampshire Snowmobile Museum located in Allenstown, New Hampshire, is the first—and only—state-sponsored snowmobile museum in the country. *And hopefully the last.*

❯ "About Us," New Hampshire Snowmobile Museum Association, *www.nhsnowmobilemuseum.com.*

The John Gorrie Museum State Park in Apalachicola, Florida, was built to honor the man who built one of Florida's most beloved inventions—the air conditioner. Visitors can view a replica of his ice-making machine, which he used to cool the rooms of patients suffering from yellow fever. *Thanks to him, Florida is a slightly less miserable place in which to live. Very slightly.*

❯ "John Gorrie Museum State Park," Florida Sate Parks, *www.floridastateparks.org.*

Missouri's Glore Psychiatric Museum is home to scores of artwork produced by patients at St. Joseph State Hospital. Possibly the strangest exhibited work is a mosaic created using 1,446 objects removed from the stomach of a patient with compulsive swallowing disorder. *Apparently you really can throw up on a canvas and call it art.*

❯ Jacopo della Quercia, "The 7 Most Horrifying Museums on Earth," *Cracked*, August 16, 2010, *www.cracked.com.*

Tucked into a corner of Hartford, Connecticut, sits the state's Trash Museum. Attractions include a one-ton Trash-o-saurus constructed out of recycled materials, an old-fashioned town dump, and a giant compost pile. *Common mistake. There's no museum; it's actually just part of the city.*

❯ "10 Strange and Obscure American Museums," Neatorama, April 6, 2007, *www.neatorama.com.*

The Carbon County Museum in Rawlins, Wyoming,

proudly displays a pair of shoes made from the skin of the notorious nineteenth-century criminal Big Nose George Parrott. *Don't knock human leather until you've tried it.*

❯ "Top 10 Shocking Historical Beliefs and Practices," Listverse, November 23, 2010, *www.listverse.com.*

The world's only ventriloquist museum resides in Fort Mitchell, Kentucky. The Vent Haven Ventriloquist Museum is open to the public, but guests must make an appointment to view the hundreds of puppets of all shapes and sizes that line the walls. *Don't worry; almost all of the dolls are completely harmless and not possessed in any way.*

❯ John Fiuffo, "Weird Roadside Attractions," *Forbes*, November 23, 2010, *www.Forbes.com.*

All new FBI agents must take a trip to the U.S. Holocaust Memorial Museum to "see firsthand what can happen when law enforcement fails to protect individuals." *Don't worry, there's an ice cream social after to break the tension.*

> "Working For the FBI," Federal Bureau of Investigation, *www.fbi.gov.*

The United States is home to two separate scale models of the *Titanic* that double as museums. One is located in Branson, Missouri, while the other is in Pigeon Forge, Tennessee. *Each is complete with an iceberg and a false sense of security.*

> "Welcome, Titanic: World's Largest Museum Attraction," *www.titanicattraction.com.*

The JAARS Museum of the Alphabet in Waxhaw, North Carolina, contains written examples produced by thousands of different cultures throughout history. However, there are still some 2,000 languages that have no corresponding alphabet. Curators for the museum hope to devise alphabets for all of the world's remaining oral languages by the year 2025. *Dream big, North Carolina. Dream big.*

> "JAARS Museum of the Alphabet Contributes to the Opening of the National Museum of Language," Christian News Wire, *www.christiannewswire.com.*

In 2011, an arsonist set fire to Mr. Ed's Elephant Museum in Franklin Township, Pennsylvania, destroying 2,000 of the museum's 10,000 elephant figurines and collectibles. Thanks to the efforts of local volunteers, the museum was soon back up and running complete with a new mosaic constructed from pieces of damaged elephant memorabilia. *Foolish arsonist. You can't kill crazy with fire.*

❭ Craig Layne, "Mr. Ed's Elephant Museum Rises from the Ashes," Fox 43, February 5, 2011, *www.fox43.com*.

Although people normally associate bananas with tropical climates, that didn't stop Ann Mitchell Lovell from opening the Washington Banana Museum in Auburn, Washington. Over the years, Lovell has acquired some 4,000 banana-related artifacts, many of which she displays at the museum. *Eccentricity laughs in the face of logic.*

❭ Deanna Hyland, "9 Unusual Food Museums That Amuse and Educate," *BootsnAll*, November 16, 2009, *www.bootsnall.com*.

Since its opening in 1992, the Roswell UFO Museum and Research Center—devoted to uncovering the truth about alien encounters—has outgrown two locations in the small New Mexico town. About 150,000 alien enthusiasts, skeptics, and curious guests visit the museum each year. *For the hundredth time, it was a weather balloon . . . piloted by midgets with leprosy who had really big eyes and communicated in a language that only they could understand.*

❭ "Museum History," UFO Museum and Research Center," *www.roswellufomuseum.com*.

In 1856, famed showman P. T. Barnum intrigued customers with promises of a six-foot-tall man eating chicken. When they arrived at the American Museum in New York City to see for themselves, they got exactly what they paid for—a six-foot-tall man eating chicken wings. *See kids, grammar is important.*

> Richard Gibbons, "The Motley Fool," October 3, 2006, *www.fool.com.*

The Elvis is Alive Museum first opened its doors in 1990 in Wright City, Missouri. Until it closed in 2007, the museum contained documents, photographs, and other artifacts procured after the singer's death that provide what many believe is indisputable proof that the King still lives on. *He's as dead as the hundred pounds of bacon that killed him.*

> "Museum Info," The Elvis is Alive Museum, *www.theelvisisalivemuseum.com.*

In 2008, a hot dog vendor in New York City bid $643,000 for the rights to sell wieners at two locations outside the entrance to the Metropolitan Museum of Art. Unfortunately, he couldn't sell enough product to keep up with the monthly payments. *His accountant shouldn't be fired. He should be shot.*

> Leslie Albrecht, "Hot Dog Vendors Pay Top Dollar in Central Park," Yahoo! News, April 6, 2011, *www.news.yahoo.com.*

Visitors to Fall River, Massachusetts, with a penchant for the macabre might want to consider staying at the Lizzie Borden Bed and Breakfast and Museum. The small home was the site of a gruesome double homicide when Andrew J. Borden and his wife were killed with a hatchet in 1892. *I don't believe in ghosts, and I'd still never stay there.*

> "Lizzie Borden Bed & Breakfast—History," Lizzie Borden Bed and Breakfast, *www.lizzie-borden.com.*

The Drug Enforcement Agency has its own museum in Arlington, Virginia, where the exhibits detail the history of drug addiction in the United States. *Oh, please, let there be samples.*

❯ "About Us," Drug Enforcement Agency Museum, *www.deamuseum.org*.

If you are afraid of bugs, you may want to steer clear of Plano, Texas, home to the Cockroach Hall of Fame. The "museum" is attached to the Pest Shop, a local store, and contains specimens dressed as celebrities and historical figures. *If it should happen to burn to the ground suddenly someday, I can assure you it was for the good of humanity.*

❯ Saul Rubin, *Offbeat Museums: The Collections and Curators of America's Most Unusual Museums* (Santa Monica Press, 1997), 190.

While most museums tout the successes of a particular field, the Museum of Questionable Medical Devices in St. Paul, Minnesota, focused on the failures. Until its closing in January 2002, visitors could view such medical tragedies as the Nemectron Machine, which "normalized" breasts using a series of metal rings. *If people were stupid enough to pay to use these things, I'm not sure they qualify as "failures."*

❯ Alex, "10 Strange and Obscure American Museums," Neatorama, April 6, 2007, *www.neatorama.com*.

The Mustard Museum in Mount Horeb, Wisconsin, is home to more than 5,000 individual jars from all over the world, as well as samples from all fifty states. *If there isn't a hot dog museum next door, I have lost all faith in humanity.*

❯ Deanna Hyland, "9 Unusual Food Museums That Amuse and Educate," *BootsnAll*, November 16, 2009, *www.bootsnall.com*.

United States presidents are permitted to borrow works of art from various Smithsonian museums to decorate the White House. The only caveat being that they may not select anything currently on public display at the Smithsonian. *Where's the fun if you can't steal from your constituents?*

> Carol Vogel, "A Bold and Modern White House," *The New York Times*, October 7, 2009, www.nytimes.com.

When Barack Obama took office, he and his wife Michelle selected some forty-five pieces from various museums to adorn the White House walls. Most were modern art pieces, but the couple did select a sculpture by French Impressionist Edgar Degas. *I'd grab every* Calvin and Hobbes *cartoon ever printed and turn the Situation Room into a giant comic strip.*

> Carol Vogel, "A Bold and Modern White House," *The New York Times*, www.nytimes.com.

The prosthetic leg of Mexican general Antonio Lopez de Santa Anna was taken by American troops during the Mexican-American war. Despite repeated requests from the Mexican government for its return, it currently resides at the Illinois State Military Museum. *If there's one thing we're good at, it's stealing stuff and claiming we own it now.*

> "Captured Leg of Santa Anna, *Roadside America*, www.roadsideamerica.com.

Since opening in 2002, the Museum of Sex in New York City has serviced thousands of curious visitors every day. The museum includes clips from pornographic films and examples of sex toys, as well as models of male and female anatomies with signs that read, "Touch gently." *If you didn't spot the pun, you are a better person than most.*

> Neil Genzlinger, "You Can Do That on a Sunday?" *The New York Times*, www.nytimes.com.

The They Also Ran Gallery is a museum attached to the First State Bank of Norton, Kansas, that houses portraits of unsuccessful contenders for the office of president of the United States. *If you have the means to run for president, it's hard to feel sorry for you.*

❯ Michelle Lovric, *Cowgirls, Cockroaches and Celebrity Lingerie: The World's Most Unusual Museums* (Totem Books, 2008), 179.

The original Museum of Bad Art (or MOBA) resides in the basement of Massachusetts's Dedham Community Theater—just outside the men's room. According to the museum, "the nearby flushing helps maintain a uniform humidity." *If you listen close, you can hear the sobs of the featured artists.*

❯ "About Moba," Museum of Bad Art, *www.museumofbadart.org*.

In 1906, curators at the Bronx Zoo briefly exhibited a Congolese pygmy named Ota Benga in the zoo's Monkey House. *In their defense, they were huge racists at the time.*

❯ Mitch Keller, "The Scandal at the Zoo," *The New York Times*, August 6, 2006, *www.nytimes.com*.

The most popular exhibit at the National Museum of Health & Medicine in Washington, D.C., is almost certainly the one devoted to Abraham Lincoln. Not only can guests view pieces of the president's shattered skull, but they can also see the bullet that ultimately caused his death. *If you squint hard enough, you can see the ghost of John Wilkes Booth giving two thumbs up.*

❯ "Exhibits," National Museum of Health & Medicine, *www.nmhm.washingtondc.museum*.

The Dayton C. Miller Flute

Collection at the Library of Congress is home to some 1,700 flutes and other wind instruments, making it the largest such collection in the world. *USA! USA!*

> "Dayton C. Miller Flute Collection," Library of Congress, *www.memory.loc.gov*.

The Kansas Barbed Wire Museum is exactly what it sounds like—an entire museum devoted to barbed wire. The building houses more than 2,000 different varieties of barbed wire. *It also doubles as a prison.*

> Jami Frater, *The Ultimate Book of Top Ten Lists: A Mind-Boggling Collection of Fun, Fascinating and Bizarre Facts on Movies, Music, Sports, Crime, Celebrities, History, Trivia and More* (Ulysses Press, 2009), 21.

The aptly named Museum of Death in San Diego, California, boasts the world's largest collection of artwork produced by serial killers, photos from famous murder scenes, a collection of body bags and coffins, and replicas of execution devices. *It makes for a great punishment trip if your kids have been misbehaving.*

> "Museum Info," The Museum of Death, *www.museumofdeath.net*.

In November 2011, germaphobes around the country got the first museum specifically for them in the form of the Museum of Clean in Pocatello, Idaho. Visitors can view everything from cleaning-related art to antique vacuum cleaners and even a timeline of toilet seats. *Just remember to wash your eyes every time you look at a new exhibit.*

❯ Jake Taylor, "Museum of Clean Opens Its Doors," *Local News 8*, November 18, 2011, *www.localnews8.com.*

When Elizabeth Tashjian first opened the Nut Museum in 1972, admission was only one nut (of any variety). She later raised her prices to $3—and one nut. *Laugh all you want, it won't be so funny when there's a nut shortage and you never bothered to stockpile.*

❯ Douglas Martin, "Elizabeth Tashjian, 94, an Expert on Nuts, Dies," *The New York Times*, February 4, 2007, *www.nytimes.com.*

The Lambert Castle Museum in Paterson, New Jersey, is home to one of the world's largest collections of spoons. The majority of the 5,400 spoons were donated by Bertha Schaefer-Koempel, a Paterson native and world traveler who donated her collection when she died in 1966. *Must . . . Not . . . Make . . . Alanis . . . Morissette . . . Joke.*

❯ Richard Cowen, "About 5,400 Spoonfuls of History at Museum," *The Bergen Record*, June 11, 2010, *www.north jersey.com.*

Boston's Isabella Stewart Gardner museum offers free admission to anyone named Isabella. *My daughter's going to be really pissed when she finds out I named her to save money on museum admission.*

❯ "Isabella's Free . . . Forever," Isabella Stewart Gardner Museum, *www.gardnermuseum .org.*

Visitors to Austin, Minnesota, can look forward to a museum containing 16,500 feet of space devoted to all things SPAM. Guests can peruse old advertisements, videos, and even visit the gift shop to buy SPAM memorabilia. *Or you could just hit yourself in the head with a spoon for two hours. It's up to you.*

❯ Deanna Hyland, "9 Unusual Food Museums That Amuse and Educate," *BootsnAll*, November 16, 2009, *www.bootsnall.com.*

The National Farm Toy Museum located in Dyersville, Iowa, is home to more than 30,000 miniature versions of farm equipment. *Parents, if you love your children, don't buy them farm toys.*

❯ "About Us," National Farm Toy Museum, *www.nationalfarmtoy museum.com.*

The Museum of Menstruation in New Carrollton, Maryland, was run by a lone man, Harry Finley, out of his basement until he had to close his doors in 1999. Due to insurance concerns associated with guests visiting his personal home, he is searching for a public venue to display his collection of feminine hygiene products throughout the ages. *Plenty of men have creepy collections in their basements. We just don't talk about them.*

❯ "Museum of Menstruation," *Roadside America, www.roadsideamerica.com.*

When self-proclaimed button king Dalton Stevens passed away, more than 600,000 buttons lined his hearse. Both the hearse and his similarly decorated coffin are on display at the Button Museum in Bishopville, South Carolina. *Proof that crazy is immortal.*

❯ Joshua Gee, *Encyclopedia Horrifica* (Scholastic, 2007), 126.

Visits to the Schwenksville, Pennsylvania's Museum of Nostalgia can be made only by appointment. While the museum does not have a phone on site, inquiries can be made at John's Old School New Skool Barber Shop in town. *Remember that time we didn't visit the Schwenksville Museum of Nostalgia? That was awesome.*

> "Schwenksville, Pennsylvania —Schwenksville Museum of Nostalgia," *Roadside America*, www.roadsideamerica.com.

In 2010, talk show host Oprah Winfrey donated a collection of 700 black angels to the Angel Museum in Beloit, Wisconsin. She acquired her vast collection after wondering aloud during a 1998 taping of her show whether black angels existed. In response, her fans sent her hundreds of black angel figurines. *Dear fans, I wonder if bags full of $1,000,000 in unmarked, nonsequential bills exist.*

> "Oprah Donates 700 Black Angels to Angel Museum," *Essence*, June 6, 2010, www.essence.com.

The only piece in the Angel Museum that does not possess wings is a figurine of Rosa Parks, who museum director Ruth Carlson considers to be her own personal angel. *Wherever Rosa Parks is now, I can assure you she spends very little of eternity hanging out in Wisconsin.*

> "Oprah Donates 700 Black Angels to Angel Museum," *Essence*, June 6, 2010, www.essence.com.

The Presidential Pet Museum opened its doors in 1999 and currently houses more than 500 artifacts related to pets kept by former presidents. Along with the usual photos and old collars, the museum also has some stranger exhibits like a portrait of Ronald Reagan's dog Lucky made from her own hair. *See, presidents are crazy too, just like you and me.*

> Michelle Lovric, *Cowgirls, Cockroaches and Celebrity Lingerie: The World's Most Unusual Museums* (Totem Books, 2008), 92.

The Money Museum attached to the Federal Reserve Bank of Chicago contains a large cube containing $1 million in $1 bills. *Sadistic challenge: You can keep all the money in the cube, but only if you can count it all accurately. If you lose count at any point, you get nothing.*

> Rachel Rice, "Rich Find Inside the Federal Reserve Bank of Chicago: a Money Museum," *Chicago Sun-Times*, September 24, 2011, *www.suntimes.com*.

The International Spy Museum in Washington, D.C., is home to more than 600 gadgets, weapons, listening devices, and hidden cameras used in the art of espionage thoughout the world. Before guests enter the museum, they are given a false identity as well as a secret mission that they are asked to perform during their visit. *The entire museum is a front to recruit young spies.*

> Rachel Cooper, "International Spy Museum in Washington, D.C.," About.com, *www.about.com*.

The Library of Natural Sounds in Ithaca, New York, stores more than 100,000 recordings obtained out in the wild. The museum contains everything from common sounds like waves crashing on the shoreline to more obscure recordings like the sound of ants kicking. *The sound of a hippo farting in the Congo on New Year's Day is particularly exquisite.*

> Sheila De La Rosa, *The Encyclopedia of Weird* (Torkids, 2005), 34.

Louisiana's UCM Museum (pronounced you-see-um) is billed as "Louisiana's most eccentric museum." The museum features everything from a collection of broken pottery dubbed "The House of Shards," to Buford the Bassigator, a creature that is part bass, part alligator. *There are no stupid museums, just stupid people willing to pay money to visit them.*

> Eric Peterson, "4 Paranormal and Other Strange Roadside Attractions," The Learning Channel, *www.tlc.howstuffworks.com*.

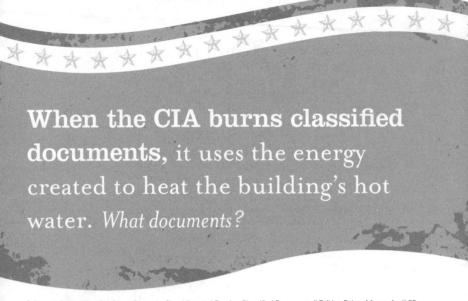

When the CIA burns classified documents, it uses the energy created to heat the building's hot water. *What documents?*

> Ryan J. Reilly, "The CIA Saves Power by Shredding and Burning Classified Documents," Talking Points Memo, April 22, 2011, *www.talkingpointsmemo.com.*

Every room in Ray Bandar's San Francisco home, save his bedroom, is almost completely covered with animal bones. He currently possesses at least 7,000 skulls, many of which are featured in the California Academy of Sciences "Skulls" exhibit. *This man needs to get laid. Stat!*

> Patricia Yollin, "The Bone Collector," *San Francisco Chronicle*, January 20, 2007, *www.sfgate .com.*

The motto of the National Museum of Funeral History is, "Any day above ground is a good one." *Unless of course you enjoy spelunking. Or are allergic to the sun. Or are a Mole Person.*

> "10 Strange and Obscure American Museums," Neatorama, April 6, 2007, *www.neatorama.com.*

Until it was moved in 2006, Marvin Johnson's Gourd Museum was housed entirely in a small building outside of his Angier, North Carolina, home. Notable pieces included a rendition of the Last Supper made from gourd seeds, a gourd replica of the orca whale Shamu, and a functioning gourd xylophone. *What happened to collecting normal things, like pocket lint in the shape of Jesus?*

❯ Saul Rubin, *Offbeat Museums: The Collections and Curators of America's Most Unusual Museums* (Santa Monica Press, 1997), 206.

Visitors to Philadelphia's Mütter Museum come from far and wide to view its collection of strange medical oddities. Aside from its famed "wall of swallowed objects," the museum possesses the thorax of John Wilkes Booth and a tumor removed from Grover Cleveland. *When I inevitably wind up there, it's a shame I won't be alive to enjoy it.*

❯ "Mutter Museum," *Roadside America*, www.roadsideamerica .com.

Leila's Hair Museum in Independence, Missouri, isn't simply a stockpile of famous locks of hair; it's one of the largest collections of hair art in the world! Retired cosmetologist and founder Leila Cohoon has more than 2,000 pieces of hair-centric jewelry dating as far back as 1680. *Who is weirder—the person who collects hair, or the person who pays to see it?*

❯ Saul Rubin, *Offbeat Museums: The Collections and Curators of America's Most Unusual Museums* (Santa Monica Press, 1997), 84.

The Mount Angel Abbey Museum in St. Benedict, Oregon, is home to the world's largest hog hairball, which sits in a glass case alongside taxidermy specimens of six-legged stuffed cows. *Would you rather they put it next to the concession stand?*

❯ Sarah Mirk, "How to Spend a Weekend Finding the World's (or at Least Oregon's) Largest Pig Hairball," *The Portland Mercury*, June 2, 2010, www.blogtown.portlandmercury.com.

Barney Smith's Toilet Seat Art Museum in Alamo Heights, Texas, houses 645 different works of art etched onto toilet seats. Ironically, the museum does not have a bathroom. *You don't really need a bathroom if you don't have visitors.*

> John Kelso, *Texas Curiosities: Quirky Characters, Roadside Oddities & Other Offbeat Stuff* (Globe Pequot, 2000), 266–267.

The price of admission to the Museum of Salt and Pepper Shakers in Gatlinburg, Tennessee, is only $3 for adults, which goes toward the purchase of any salt and pepper shaker from the gift shop. *You'd be a fool not to go.*

> "History," The Salt and Pepper Shaker Museum, *www.thesalt andpeppershakermuseum.com.*

There are more than 500 herbal cures on display at the Kam Wah Chung & Co. Museum in John Day, Oregon. Before it was converted into a museum, the Chinese apothecary who owned and operated the store treated his patients with everything from chicken gizzards and tiger bones to bear paws and deer antlers. *You'd be amazed what can be cured by a good old-fashioned vomit session.*

> Saul Rubin, *Offbeat Museums: The Collections and Curators of America's Most Unusual Museums* (Santa Monica Press, 1997), 114.

⇛ CHAPTER 8 ⇚

Catacombs, Hidden Cities, and the Chrysler Building's Secret Spire

Mind-Blowing Constructions to Astound

Until I started researching this book, I could have thought of few things less interesting than a building. I mean, there isn't much exciting about a few steel girders filled in with some concrete.

As it turns out, I was wrong. Very wrong. It wasn't long before I found myself waist-deep in secret underground tunnels used to kidnap unsuspecting Oregonians. Once I uncovered the reclusive "Mole People" living in the New York City subway system, I was hooked. And by the time you're done with this chapter, hopefully you will be convinced that America's skyscrapers, monuments, and government buildings are just as creepy as the aliens who may or may not have built some of them.

The twelve-story Mountain Bay Plaza building in Mountain View, California, was built from the top down. Workers constructed each floor at ground level and then hoisted it up to the top.

Because only sissies worry about gravity.

❭ Daniel DeBolt, "From 'Dog City' to Cash Cow," *Mountain View Voice*, January 2, 2009, *www.mv-voice.com.*

Below the Freedom Tunnel subway entrance near 125th Street and Riverside Park in New York City live a group of subterranean dwellers known as "Mole People." The group functions almost completely underground, and lives in shantytown structures that are routinely bulldozed by the city. *Bring along a Zippo, they might make you their God.*

❭ Alan Ishac and Cari Jackson, *The Guide to Odd New York: Unusual Places, Weird Attractions and the City's Most Curious Sights* (Allan Ishac LLC, 2010), 71.

When architect William Van Alen learned of another planned skyscraper that would be taller than his Chrysler Building—which was already under construction—he ordered a 125-foot spire to be built in secret within the building. It would only be affixed to the roof after plans for the rival building were finalized. *Because second place is just the first loser.*

❭ Neal Bascomb, "For the Architect, a Height Never Again to Be Scaled," *The New York Times*, May 26, 2005, *www.nytimes.com.*

When it was finished in May 1930, the Chrysler Building stood 1,046 feet, making it the tallest man-made structure at the time. The Empire State Building would steal that honor less than a year later. *"Quick boys, get the other spire!"*

❯ Neal Bascomb, "For the Architect, a Height Never Again to Be Scaled," *The New York Times*, May 26, 2005, www.nytimes.com.

There is a **Best Buy** electronics store housed inside the Pentagon. *God forbid the government should be without their $100 HDMI cables.*

❯ Dave McKenna, "Snyder Still Exploiting Military/Grid-iron Complex," *Washington City Paper*, July 24, 2010, www.washingtoncitypaper.com.

Lady Liberty wears a size 879 sandal and has a thirty-five-foot waistline. *False. The sandals aren't real shoes, they're just copper. This message brought to you courtesy of Captain Buzz Killington.*

❯ "20 Facts About the Statue of Liberty," How Stuff Works, www.history.howstuffworks.com.

More than 650 feet below the surface of Hutchinson, Kansas, sits Underground Vaults and Storage, the ultimate in secure repositories. The site is home to such valuables as original reels of *The Wizard of Oz* and *Gone with the Wind* as well as a Stradivarius violin. *Finally, a impenetrable fortress worthy of my vintage POG collection.*

> Sheila De La Rosa, *The Encyclopedia of Weird* (Torkids, 2005), 48.

Each year, several couples are permitted to exchange wedding vows on the eightieth floor of the Empire State Building. Doing so lands them in the Empire State Building Wedding Club, which entitles them to free admission to the observatories every Valentine's Day. *Free admission? Gee, how big of them.*

> Pamela Skillings, "The Empire State Building," About.com, *www.manhattan.about.com.*

There is a **full-scale replica** of the U.S. Capitol Building in a Jiangsu provincial village in China. *Good to know we have a plan B when the aliens attack.*

> "China's Richest Village Builds Replicas of Famous Architectures," Cultural China, *www.hotnews.cultural-china.com.*

Piggy banks are so shaped to honor Wilbur Chapman of White Cloud, Kansas, who sold his prize pig to raise money for a leper colony in 1910. A monument that pays tribute to his sacrifice sits in the courtyard of the Community Christian Church on Main Street. *Gotta love how we think in America, "Screw the pig, what a brave little boy!"*

> Bridget Gleeson, "America's Strangest Monuments," AOL Travel, November 10, 2009, *www.travel.aol.com.*

Rather than settle for an ordinary office building, the CEO of the Longaberger basket company in Newark, Ohio, designed the headquarters as a perfect replica of the company's Medium Market Basket. The massive handles are attached to the structure with copper and wooden rivets, and the gold-leaf-plated tags each weigh 725 pounds. *Half the staff had to be laid off to realize his dream, but it was worth it.*

❯ Destinations: Home Office, Longaberger, *www.longaberger.com.*

Just north of Homestead, Florida, sits Coral Castle, a massive limestone structure built by Edward Leedskalnin in the early twentieth century. With some of the stones being larger than those at Stonehenge, nobody is sure how he managed to build it over twenty-eight years all by himself. Some residents claimed they saw him raise the stones with balloons while others insist he used magical powers to levitate them. *He did have supernatural abilities. The magical power of money.*

❯ Nathan Birch, "7 Insane True Stories Behind the World's Most WTF Houses," *Cracked,* December 4, 2009, *www.cracked.com.*

When building the United States Treasury Building, due to his disdain for Congress President Andrew Jackson insisted it be built so that the main building blocked his view of the Capitol. *I feel I would have liked him.*

❯ "U.S. Treasury Building," D Guides, *www.dguides.com.*

In January of 2001, a group of rogue artists erected a nine-foot-tall monolith in Seattle identical to the one depicted in the film *2001: A Space Odyssey.* The structure was made entirely of steel and weighed 500 pounds. *I kind of want to leave a leg bone at its feet, just to see what happens.*

❯ Associated Press, "Mysterious Monolith Appears in Seattle," *USA Today,* January 2, 2001, *www.usatoday.com.*

Walt Disney initially intended his famous EPCOT Center to serve as the model for a larger utopian society. The name stands for Experimental Prototype Community of Tomorrow. Had he realized his dream, 20,000 people could have lived in his climate-controlled paradise. *I'd rather live on Pleasure Island.*

❯ John Jeremiah Sullivan, "You Blow My Mind. Hey, Mickey!" *The New York Times,* June 8, 2011, *www.nytimes.com.*

Rockport, Massachusetts, is home to the Paper House, made almost entirely out of pasted, coated, or rolled-up newspapers. The only exceptions are the framework, floorboards, and shingles. *I'm also made entirely out of paper. Except my hair, skin, bones, muscle, organs, nails, and teeth.*

❯ John Fiuffo, "Weird Roadside Attractions," *Forbes,* November 23, 2010, *www.Forbes.com.*

The Run-Over Fireman Monument in Washington, D.C., was erected to honor Benjamin Grenup, a local fireman killed in the line of duty on May 6, 1856. The memorial recreates—in graphic detail—the moment when he was run over by a wayward firetruck. *I'm not saying you deserved to die if you couldn't outrun a horse-drawn firetruck, but you definitely didn't deserve to procreate.*

❯ Bridget Gleeson, "America's Strangest Monuments," AOL Travel, November 10, 2009, *www.travel.aol.com.*

On December 2, 1979, Elvita Adams flung herself from the Empire State Building, only to be blown into an open window on the eighty-fifth floor. *If at first you don't succeed . . .*

> George H. Douglas, *Skyscrapers: A Social History of the Very Tall Building in America* (McFarland & Co., 2004), 173.

The CIA is home to many mysteries, one of the most famous of which sits right in the courtyard of its Virginia headquarters. Called "Kryptos," the sculpture is actually a series of four encrypted messages, only three of which have ever been solved. *If the documentary* A Christmas Story *has taught me anything, the message is "Be sure to drink your Ovaltine."*

> John Schwartz, "Clues to Stubborn Secret in C.I.A.'s Backyard," *The New York Times*, November 20, 2010, *www.nytimes.com*.

London Bridge no longer spans the River Thames in London, nor does it reside anywhere in England. It was transported in 1971, piece by piece, to its current home in Lake Havasu City, Arizona. *If you can't build your own culture, buy it.*

> Marc Lacy, "A Red-Letter Day, and a Party to Match," *The New York Times*, October 12, 2011, *www.nytimes.com*.

America's only memorial to honor deceased circus performers can be found inside a cemetery in Colma, California. The Memorial for Circus Showfolks of America consists of a large yellow clown face surrounded by a big top tent and a merry-go-round. *If you love clowns, it's touching. If you hate clowns, they're dead. Everybody wins.*

> Bridget Gleeson, "America's Strangest Monuments," AOL Travel, November 10, 2009, *www.travel.aol.com*.

Beneath the keystone of the St. Louis Arch sits a 1963 time capsule containing the signatures of 762,000 St. Louis students. *Imagine that. In 1963 there were 762,000 literate children in St. Louis.*

❯ Mary Delach Leonard, "Wow! At 40, Shining Arch Still Is Beacon to Visitors," *St. Louis Post-Dispatch*, October 19, 2005, *www.stltoday.com.*

When not being used to allow pedestrians and cyclists to cross the Sacramento River in Redding, California, the aptly named Sundial Bridge doubles as a giant timepiece. The bridge's 217-foot support tower points due north, and its shadow can be used to calculate the time. *In case your watch breaks, your cell phone dies, and everyone else on earth disappears.*

❯ Bobby Caina Calvan, "Bridge Unites Parkland, Divides Town," *The Boston Globe*, April 5, 2004, *www.boston.com.*

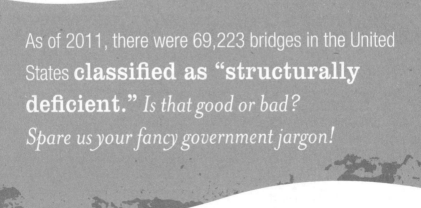

As of 2011, there were 69,223 bridges in the United States **classified as "structurally deficient."** *Is that good or bad? Spare us your fancy government jargon!*

❯ Alex Goldmark, "One in Nine Bridges in America 'Structurally Deficient, Potentially Dangerous,'" Transportation Nation, March 30, 2011, *www.transportationnation.org.*

It took artist Mark Perez nearly fifteen years, but in 2010 he unveiled a giant version of the popular Mousetrap game at the World Maker Faire in Queens, New York. The structure weighed 50,000 pounds and included a 350-pound bathtub, a 30-foot crane, a two-ton safe, and a host of other dangerous objects. *Want.*

❯ Caroline McCarthy, "At Maker Faire, Giant Mousetrap Crushes a Taxi," Cnet, September 26, 2010, *www.cnet.com.*

Each time Perez's team makes an appearance with their giant Mousetrap game, it takes them five days to assemble and two days to take down. *Longer if Perez's older brother shows up and kicks the board over.*

❯ Caroline McCarthy, "At Maker Faire, Giant Mousetrap Crushes a Taxi," Cnet, September 26, 2010, *www.cnet.com.*

In the outskirts of Alliance, Nebraska, sits Carhenge, an exact recreation of England's Stonehenge constructed from thirty-eight classic American automobiles. The replica has a diameter of ninety-six feet with some of the cars buried up to five feet in the earth to support the structure. *It may be stupid, but that's pretty damned impressive.*

❯ "Carhenge History," Carhenge.com, *www.carhenge.com.*

Only eleven workers died during the construction of the Golden Gate Bridge in the 1930s, a safety record at the time. *It would have been ten, but Jeff just had to be the first person to jump off.*

❯ Charlotte Lowe, *The Utterly, Completely, and Totally Useless Fact-O-Pedia: A Startling Collection of Over 1,000 Things You'll Never Need to Know* (Skyhorse Publishing, 2011).

Visitors to Boston, Massachusetts, who cross Massachusetts Avenue bridges from Boston to Cambridge may notice strange markings at intervals spanning the structure. The markers are relics from a 1958 MIT fraternity prank in which members laid their shortest pledge, Oliver Smoot, on the ground and measured the bridge in Smoot body lengths, marking the distance every ten "Smoots." *And you thought frats were for cool kids.*

❯ David A. Fahrenthold, "The Measure of This Man Is in the Smoot," *The Washington Post*, December 8, 2005, *www.washingtonpost.com.*

Boston's Massachusetts Avenue bridge is 364.4 Smoots—and one ear—long. *Nerds are nothing if not precise.*

❯ David A. Fahrenthold, "The Measure of This Man Is in the Smoot," *The Washington Post*, December 8, 2005, *www.washingtonpost.com.*

When he got sick of mowing his lawn, Houston resident John Milkovisch opted to encase marbles, rocks, and various knickknacks in concrete to replace the grass on his property. Now known as "The Beer Can House," Milkovisch's property also sports 50,000 cans' worth of aluminum siding, wind chimes, and other strange decorations. *It's only ugly if you happen to have eyes.*

❯ Nathan Birch, "7 Insane True Stories Behind the World's Most WTF Houses," *Cracked*, December 4, 2009, *www.cracked.com.*

New York City has 186 skyscrapers. It is second only to Hong Kong, which has 195. *It's not that China is better than the United States .They're just less bad at being good at stuff.*

❯ Russell Ash, *Firefly's World of Facts* (Firefly Books, 2007), 203.

The never-used Cincinnati subway system is the largest abandoned subway in the United States. The project was started in 1920 and it would cost an estimated $19 million today to fill in the unused tunnels. *Just build a youth rec center down there and call it a day.*

❯ "Cincinnati Considers Options for Decades-Old Unfinished Subway," News5 WLWT, December 6, 2007, *www.wlwt.com.*

Three of the ten largest bridges

in the world are located in Louisiana. *Large people, large bridges. Makes sense.*

❯ Amanda Briney, "Longest Bridges in the World," About.com, October 7, 2011, *www.geography.about.com.*

Thanks to its unique shape, the Flatiron Building in New York City has the inherent ability to direct wind gusts and lift women's dresses as they walk by. In the early 1900s, men frequently gathered at the building's location at 5th Avenue and 23rd Street to enjoy the show. *Modern men are more civilized. Now we have Internet porn.*

❯ Richard Grigonis, "The Flatiron Building, New York City," Interesting America, January 3, 2011, *www.interestingamerica.com.*

In 1931, at least twenty-four famous architects arrived at the Beaux-Arts Ball dressed as the buildings they had designed. Among them were William Van Alen as the Chrysler Building, Leonard Schultze as the Waldorf-Astoria, and Ralph Walker as the Wall Street Building. *Modesty is overrated anyway.*

❯ Christopher Gray, "A New Age of Architecture Ushered in Financial Gloom," *The New York Times*, January 1, 2006, *www.nytimes.com.*

Sixty-three feet below the surface of the ocean off the coast of Florida rests Aquarius, an underwater laboratory where researchers work for up to ten days at a time. The facility contains six bunks, a shower and toilet, trash compactor, refrigerator, and even air conditioning. *Nice to know people dwelling underwater live better than I do.*

❯ "About Aquarius," Aquarius Reef Base, *www.aquarius .uncw.edu.*

The last meal of Timothy McVeigh, the terrorist responsible for the 1995 Oklahoma City bombings, consisted of two pints of mint chocolate chip ice cream. *Not sure if this makes me like that flavor more or less.*

❯ Ian Harrison, *Take Me to Your Leader* (Dorling Kindersley Ltd., 2007), 345.

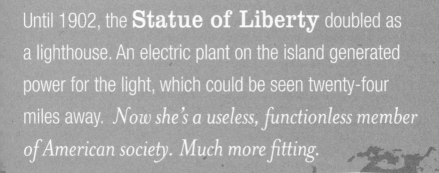

Until 1902, the **Statue of Liberty** doubled as a lighthouse. An electric plant on the island generated power for the light, which could be seen twenty-four miles away. *Now she's a useless, functionless member of American society. Much more fitting.*

❯ "20 Facts About the Statue of Liberty," How Stuff Works, *www.history.howstuffworks.com.*

It took 467 cement trucks about twelve hours to fill the thirty-foot-deep, 120-foot-wide foundation of Seattle's Space Needle. The resulting foundation weighed 5,850 tons. *Holy sweet Goddamn.*

❯ "Mysteries Revealed," Space Needle, *www.spaceneedle.com.*

When fellow restaurateurs Tim Firnstahl and Mick McHugh could not agree on how to divide up their $16 million Seattle restaurant empire, they settled the matter with a simple coin flip—tossed from the top of the Space Needle. *Heads I win, tails you lose.*

❯ "Mysteries Revealed," Space Needle, *www.spaceneedle.com.*

The Committee Hoping for ExtraTerrestrial Encounters to Save the Earth (CHEESE) claims that the original plans for the Space Needle imply it was initially intended to be used to send transmissions to alien beings in other solar systems. *Might want to rethink that acronym.*

❯ "Mysteries Revealed," Space Needle, *www.spaceneedle.com.*

Disappointed in the lack of catacombs in the United States, Reverend Mateo Amoros decided to build his own beneath St. Joseph's Church in Newark, New Jersey, in 1937. Because state law prohibited the exhibition of real dead bodies, he instead filled his catacomb with wax replicas of famous church martyrs, inadvertently establishing the country's first wax museum. *Of course, it's in New Jersey.*

❯ "Catacombs of St. Joseph," *Roadside America, www.roadsideamerica.com.*

The blinking red light atop the Capitol Records Building in Los Angeles spells out "Hollywood" in Morse code. *Or "Oolhydolw" if you're dyslexic. And know Morse code.*

❯ "Capitol Records Building," *The New York Times*, www .travel.nytimes.com.

You don't need to travel all the way to Egypt to see pyramids. You can visit the 125-foot-tall Rainforest Pyramid in Galveston, Texas, which houses one of the world's largest indoor rainforests. *Or better yet, just fire up the laptop and you'll never have to leave your couch. It's the twenty-first century American dream.*

❯ Russell Ash, *Firefly's World of Facts* (Firefly Books, 2007), 201.

Beneath Grand Central Station lies a network of underground tracks as well as a platform with a secret entrance and an elevator straight to the Waldorf-Astoria hotel. President Franklin D. Roosevelt is said to have used them as a way to travel to New York City without being bothered by reporters. *Or Eleanor.*

❯ Pamela Skillings, "Secrets of Grand Central Terminal," About.com, www.manhattan .about.com.

Beneath the city of Portland, Oregon, reside a series of labyrinthine tunnels that nineteenth-century criminals used to kidnap unsuspecting men and women and ship them to Asia to serve as slave labor or prostitutes. This practice was known as "shanghaiing," a term that is still used today to describe obtaining by force. *Please don't call it that.*

❯ "Top 10 Most Haunted Cities in the U.S.," TopTenz.net, www .toptenz.net.

Despite the fact that the former mayor of Fort Wayne, Indiana, won a 2011 Internet poll to name the town's new building after him, town officials refused. They felt "Harry Baals Government Center" sounded inappropriate. *Reporters could not find Amanda Hugnkiss, the de facto winner, to comment.*

❯ Benjamin Lanka, "Harry Baals Building Unlikely," *The Fort Wayne Journal Gazette*, February 11, 2011, *www.journalgazette.net.*

The order of the faces in Mount Rushmore was initially intended to be (from left to right) **Jefferson, Washington, Roosevelt, and Lincoln.** When the sculptor discovered cracks in the rock while sculpting Jefferson, he simply blasted away his work and moved the third president to Washington's right. *See, dynamite does solve everything.*

❯ Sheila De La Rosa, *The Encyclopedia of Weird* (Torkids, 2005), 40.

When authorities confiscated the embalmed bodies of Jean Stevens's deceased husband and twin sister from her Pennsylvania home, the ninety-one-year-old woman did the only logical thing she could think of—she built a mausoleum next door. Authorities assure her they will return the bodies once it's completed. *Something tells me they're just trying to wait her out . . .*

❯ "Widow, 91, Builds Crypt at Home to Get Back the Confiscated Corpses of Her Loved Ones," *Daily Mail*, January 4, 2011, *www.dailymail.co.uk.*

Engineers at the Long Now Foundation plan to build a clock inside a mountain on the border of Texas and New Mexico that will be able to keep perfect time for the next 10,000 years. *Pity we won't be around to enjoy the last 9,950 years of its timekeeping majesty.*

> "How the 10,000-Year Clock Measures Time," *Technology Review*, December 15, 2011, *www.technologyreview.com*.

The top of the Empire State Building was designed to serve as a docking station for zeppelins. However, it has not once been used for that purpose. *Sort of like that condom you've kept in your pocket since high school.*

> Christopher Gray, "Not Just a Perch for King Kong," *The New York Times*, September 23, 2010, *www.nytimes.com*.

The total value of the gold held at Fort Knox, Kentucky is roughly $6.2 billion. *Or 24.8 billion Tootsie Pops.*

> "The United States Bullion Depository Fort Knox, Kentucky," United States Mint, *www.usmint.gov*.

The gold depository at Fort Knox, Kentucky, currently houses 147.3 million ounces of gold. Since its opening in 1937, no additional gold has been added and only trace amounts have been removed. *For now . . .*

> "The United States Bullion Depository Fort Knox, Kentucky," United States Mint, *www.usmint.gov*.

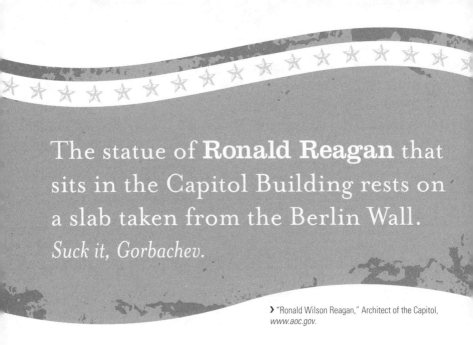

The statue of **Ronald Reagan** that sits in the Capitol Building rests on a slab taken from the Berlin Wall. *Suck it, Gorbachev.*

❯ "Ronald Wilson Reagan," Architect of the Capitol, *www.aoc.gov.*

Aside from its vast cache of gold, Fort Knox has been home to a number of important artifacts such as the Magna Carta, the Declaration of Independence, and the Articles of Confederation. *Yet they won't watch over my mint condition Garbage Pail Kids collection. Go figure.*

❯ "The United States Bullion Depository Fort Knox, Kentucky," United States Mint, *www.usmint.gov.*

The annual stealing and returning of the letter "T" from the word "Tech" affixed to the Georgia Tech Tower was a time-honored tradition until the university put a stop to the practice in 2001. Since then, students have taken to stealing smaller "t's" from various signs on campus. *Sure, steal things from a university you pay to attend. That'll show 'em.*

❯ Renee Sarzyk, "Georgia Tech Wants Stolen "T's" Back," CBS Atlanta, September 28, 2011, *www.cbsatlanta.com.*

The world's tallest monument isn't in Egypt, or China, or even in Peru. It's a 570-foot column commemorating the battle of San Jacinto near Houston, Texas. *The only problem is that once you've seen it, you're stuck in Houston.*

> Russell Ash, *Firefly's World of Facts* (Firefly Books, 2007), 201.

The government of **Abu Dhabi owns 90%** of the Chrysler Building. *They let us keep the gift shop.*

> Charles V. Bagu, "Abu Dhabi Buys 90% Stake in Chrysler Building," *The New York Times*, July 10, 2008, *www.nytimes.com.*

The Georgia Guidestones are five sixteen-foot-tall slabs of granite etched with instructions for rebuilding society in the event of an apocalypse. The stones were built by the Elberton Granite Finishing Company in 1979, although nobody knows exactly who commissioned them. *It was probably aliens, or at least funny-looking humans.*

> Randall Sullivan, "American Stonehenge: Monumental Instructions for the Post-Apocalypse," *Wired*, April 20, 2009, *www.wired.com.*

Chicago's O'Hare International Airport is the busiest airport on earth. On average, a plane lands or takes off every 42.5 seconds, which equates to about 741,000 flights a year. *Try telling that to the people waiting on the runway.*

> Pustak Mahal, *501 Astonishing Facts* (Pustak Mahal, 2010).

Reed College in Portland, Oregon, is home to the only nuclear reactor in the country run by undergraduates. *What's the worst that could happen? Oh, right . . .*

❯ "Reed Research Reactor," Reed College, *www.reed.edu.*

If two people stand at opposite ends of the arches near Grand Central Station's Oyster Bar & Restaurant and whisper, they should be able to hear one another as if they were standing face to face. The strange effect is due to the curvature of the domed ceiling, which channels the sound of the whispers. *Which can be very awkward if you are just trying to have a private moment with the wall.*

❯ Pamela Skillings, "Secrets of Grand Central Terminal," About.com, *www.manhattan .about.com.*

There are 132 rooms in the White House, thirty-two of which are bathrooms. *Who are they to tell us which rooms we can use for what? If you're peeing in it, rest assured, it is now a bathroom.*

❯ Erin Barrett and Jack Mingo, *Random Kinds Of Factness: 1001 (or So) Absolutely True Tidbits About (Mostly) Everything* (Conari Press, 2005), 6.

In 1978, architect William J. LeMessurier discovered a terrifying flaw in his 114-foot-tall Citicorp building—a seventy-mile-an-hour gust of wind could bring the entire building crashing down. During the next three months, welders worked around the clock to reinforce more than 200 bolted joints and avert disaster. *Who could have guessed a building might someday get hit by wind?*

❯ Alan Bellows, *Alien Hand Syndrome and Other Too-Weird-To-Be-True Stories* (Workman Publishing, 2009), 137.

When investors signed off on the blueprints for the Newby-McMahon Building in Wichita Falls, Texas, they were expecting a 418-foot skyscraper. What they got was a miniature version, only four stories tall. They failed to notice that the sneaky architect had drafted up the blueprints in inches instead of feet. *Who has time to read things?*

> Kaushik, "World's Littlest Skyscraper," Amusing Planet, September 19, 2011, *www.amusingplanet.com.*

The record for running up the 1,576 stairs in the Empire State Building is nine minutes and thirty-three seconds, set in 2003. *Why do people scoff in the face of technology?*

> Pamela Skillings, "The Empire State Building," About.com, *www.manhattan.about.com.*

The Golden Gate Bridge is the most popular place on earth to commit suicide. Since it opened in 1937, more than 1,300 people have leaped into San Francisco Bay to their deaths. *If you lived in San Francisco, you'd understand.*

> James Bone, "Golden Gate Bridge in San Francisco Gets Safety Net to Deter Suicides," *The Times,* October 13, 2008, *www.timesonline.co.uk.*

Only twenty-six people have ever survived a jump from the Golden Gate Bridge, putting the mortality rate around 98 percent. *They even failed at giving up.*

> Tad Friend, "Jumpers," *The New Yorker,* October 13, 2003, *www.newyorker.com.*

CHAPTER 9

From President John Quincy Adams's Pet Alligator to Pope Michael from Kansas

Bizarre People to Marvel At

A country is only as strange as its people, and, rest assured, America is ahead of the game on that front. Where else can you find a musician who dedicates his memoir to his penis in the same place as a former vice president (and current zombie)? Nowhere, that's where.

In this chapter, you will find startling truths about our most beloved celebrities and political figures, as well as shocking information about Americans you have never even heard of (and will probably wish you hadn't). But before you judge, think about this: Are their eccentricities any worse than your own?

On the day he was shot and killed at Ford's Theater, Abraham Lincoln signed into law legislation that created the Secret Service Agency, a group charged with protecting the president. *"This doesn't need to go into effect until tomorrow though. I'm just going to the theater, after all!"*

❯ Dan Lewis, "Abraham Lincoln Created the Secret Service the Day He Was Shot," Mental Floss, December 14, 2010, *www.mentalfloss.com.*

During the filming of *The African Queen* in the Congo, the entire crew fell ill with dysentery save for director John Huston and actor Humphrey Bogart. The pair refused water in favor of whiskey. *Alcohol really does fix everything.*

❯ "The African Queen—Bogart, Hepburn, and a Case of the 'Jungle Jeebies,'" *The Independent*, May 7, 2010, *www.independent.co.uk.*

Humphrey Bogart's last words were, "I should never have switched from Scotch to martinis." *Amen brother.*

❯ Jamie Frater, *Listverse.com's Ultimate Book of Bizarre Lists: Fascinating Facts and Shocking Trivia on Movies, Music, Crime, Celebrities, History, and More* (Ulysses Press, 2010), 62.

At the age of ten, Pittsburgh native William Stark lost the lens of his left eye to a wayward nail. When he recovered, he discovered his sight had actually been enhanced and certain objects, like the sun, moon, and flowers, glowed with a bluish hue. The injury had made him one of the few humans capable of detecting ultraviolet light. *A witch! Kill it with fire!*

❯ Ivan Amato, "Bird's-Eye View," *Fortune*, April 4, 2005, *www.fortune.com.*

Who has the honor of being the fattest president? Weighing in at a hefty 300 pounds, that would be President William Howard Taft. *And he didn't even have McDonald's. He had to work for his obesity.*

❯ Phyllis Goldman, *Monkeyshines on Strange and Wonderful Facts* (Monkeyshines, 1991), 28.

Despite his heftiness, Taft was also one of the longest-lived presidents, surviving to the ripe old age of seventy-four. *A nice age to strive for. Old enough for a wealth of experiences, but not so old that you're back in diapers.*

❯ Phyllis Goldman, *Monkeyshines on Strange and Wonderful Facts* (Monkeyshines, 1991), 28.

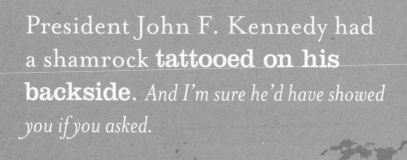

President John F. Kennedy had a shamrock **tattooed on his backside**. *And I'm sure he'd have showed you if you asked.*

❯ Dane Sherwood, Sandy Wood, and Kara Kovalchik, *The Pocket Idiot's Guide to Not So Useless Facts* (Penguin Group, 2006).

Actor Andy Garcia was born with a parasitic twin the size of a tennis ball attached to his shoulder. *Alternatively, Andy Garcia's brother was born with a baby-sized human attached to his feet. His parents chose wisely.*

> "Was Walt Disney Frozen after Death? Top 10 Celebrity Myths Debunked," *The Telegraph*, April 30, 2009, *www.telegraph.co.uk.*

Environmental activist Julia Hill once spent 738 days between 1997 and 1999 in a 600-year-old redwood tree in Northern California to prevent a lumber company from cutting it down. The company eventually relented and allowed the tree to stay, along with an additional three-acre buffer zone of surrounding trees. *And this was before occupying things was trendy.*

> Brita Belli, "Commentary: Behind the Greens: 10 Questions for Activist Julia Butterfly Hill," *E–The Environmental Magazine*, October 7, 2007, *www.emagazine.com.*

Famed American author Ernest Hemingway once wrote a story that was only six words long. It read, "For sale: Baby shoes, never worn." *Apparently brevity is the secret to sadness.*

> "Very Short Stories," *Wired*, November 2006, *www.wired.com.*

With more than 100 corsets to her name, Cathie Jung of Mystic, Connecticut, is the proud owner of the world's smallest adult waist. Her minuscule waist is just fifteen inches around, or roughly the size of a mayonnaise jar. *Before you try this at home, remember that waist size attractiveness is on a bell curve.*

> "15 World Records of Shame," Herald Daily, January 11, 2010, *www.heralddaily.com.*

On October 14, 1912, President Theodore Roosevelt was shot in the chest by a would-be assassin while giving a speech in Milwaukee. Rather than go to the hospital, he finished his speech, declaring, "It takes more than one bullet to kill a bull moose." *Big talk for a man named Teddy.*

> Scott McCabe, "Crime History: Teddy Roosevelt Shot, Gives Speech with Bullet in Chest," Washington Examiner, October 13, 2011, *www.washingtonexaminer.com.*

In 2004, authorities discovered a small shack connected to the girders and beams of a drawbridge that crossed the Chicago River. The structure—built by a local homeless man named Richard Dorsay—connected to the bridge's power lines and contained a microwave, television, space heater, and video game system. *Doesn't sound very homeless to me.*

> Associated Press, "Man Found Living Comfortably Inside Chicago Drawbridge," USA Today, December 14, 2004, *www .usatoday.com.*

Herman Webster Mudgett, better known as Dr. Henry Howard Holmes, holds the honor of being America's first documented serial killer. During the course of Chicago's 1893 World's Fair, he confessed to killing at least twenty-seven people in his self-constructed "murder castle." *Don't let the name fool you, it's actually more of a murder manor.*

> Katherine Ramsland, "H. H. Holmes: Master of Illusion," Tru TV, *www.trutv.com.*

In 2004, an intruder broke into the home of Joe Francis, creator of the *Girls Gone Wild* franchise, and forced him to perform in a homoerotic pornographic video. *It's not really okay to laugh at that, but it's close.*

> "Joe Francis," MSNBC, *www.msnbc.msn.com.*

Martha Stewart has been struck by lightning three times. *Fourth time's the charm.*

> "Stewart Lived Through Three Lightning Strikes," *San Francisco Chronicle*, April 22, 2009, *www.sfgate.com.*

When ten-year-old Dugan Smith was diagnosed with a deadly form of bone cancer in his thigh, his only concern was being able to play baseball again. To save his mobility, doctors performed an extremely rare procedure called a rotationplasty. They detached his lower leg, rotated it 180 degrees, and reattached it higher on the leg, effectively transforming his ankle into a knee that fit into a prosthetic leg. *Google at your own risk.*

> Eric Adelson, "Stunning Medical Procedure Saves a Boy's Baseball Dream," *The Post Game*, May 19, 2011, *www.thepostgame.com.*

President George Washington was a champion wrestler and long jumper. *Handy skills for a ten-year-old. Not as useful for a president.*

> Pustak Mahal, *501 Astonishing Facts* (Pustak Mahal, 2010).

After his wife severed his penis with a kitchen knife in 1993, John Wayne Bobbitt formed the band Severed Parts in an attempt to cash in on his pseudo-celebrity status. The band never took off. *He missed the eunuch craze by a few thousand years.*

> "John Wayne Bobbitt," IMDb, *www.imdb.com.*

To protect himself from the allure of prostitutes, Boston Corbett—the man who killed John Wilkes Booth—castrated himself with a pair of scissors. *He later shot himself in the head to cure his persistent migraines.*

> Eric Niderost, "Crazy Boston Corbett Killed John Wilkes Booth," Historynet, August 25, 2010, *www.historynet.com.*

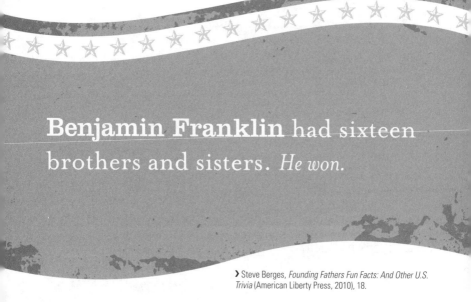

Benjamin Franklin had sixteen brothers and sisters. *He won.*

> Steve Berges, *Founding Fathers Fun Facts: And Other U.S. Trivia* (American Liberty Press, 2010), 18.

Actor Christopher Walken

worked briefly as a lion tamer when he was fifteen. *He talked them into submission.*

› "Christopher Walken," IMDb, *www.imdb.com.*

With a net worth of $336 billion dollars, John D. Rockefeller remains the wealthiest man in modern history. *I am currently number 4,333,211,443. Please buy this book and help me overtake Carrot Top.*

› "The 20 Richest People of All Time," *Business Insider, www .businessinsider.com.*

In 2006, actor William Shatner put his kidney stone up for auction to raise money for Habitat for Humanity. It sold to the online casino Golden Palace for $25,000. *I don't care whose pee-hole it came out of. It's not worth that much.*

› "Actor Shatner Sells Kidney Stone," BBC News, January 18, 2006, *www.bbc.co.uk.*

After her death in 1851, the mother of Virginia Macdonald vehemently insisted her daughter had been buried alive and demanded the remains be exhumed. Much to the family's horror, they discovered her body lying on its side with the fingers badly bitten, clear signs that the mother had been right all along. *Thank god they cleared that up several weeks too late.*

› Jamie Frater, *Listverse.com's Ultimate Book of Bizarre Lists: Fascinating Facts and Shocking Trivia on Movies, Music, Crime, Celebrities, History, and More* (Ulysses Press, 2010), 17.

To prevent the tortuous death that would arise due to an untimely burial, many coffins were outfitted with devices that would allow a mistakenly buried person to alert those topside of the error. Dubbed "safety coffins," they were popular in the nineteenth century. *Which is why I plan to be "buried" sitting on my couch with a six-pack.*

> ❯ Jamie Frater, *Listverse.com's Ultimate Book of Bizarre Lists: Fascinating Facts and Shocking Trivia on Movies, Music, Crime, Celebrities, History, and More* (Ulysses Press, 2010), 15.

Mark Wahlberg's 1992 memoir *Marky Mark* is dedicated to his penis. *I knew there was a reason I hated him.*

> ❯ "Mark Wahlberg's Penis Dedication No Longer Funny," *New York Post*, August 4, 2010, *www.nypost.com*.

During a duel in 1806, Andrew Jackson shot and killed a man who had insulted his wife and accused him of cheating on a horse race. He was never tried for murder, and the incident did little to impede his future rise to the presidency. *I mean, did we really want a president who would let that slide?*

> ❯ "May 30, 1806: Andrew Jackson Kills Charles Dickinson in Duel," History Channel, *www.history.com*.

While testing high-altitude suits for the U.S. government in 1960, pilot Joe Kittinger jumped from a balloon floating 102,800 feet above New Mexico. His freefall lasted four minutes and thirty-six seconds and reached a top speed of 614 miles per hour, a record that has yet to be beaten. *I'm going to guess that record's pretty safe for now.*

> ❯ John Tierney, "A Supersonic Jump, from 23 Miles in the Air," *The New York Times*, March 15, 2010, *www.nytimes.com*.

The honor of world's largest man belonged to American Jon Brower Minnoch (1941–1983). During his life, he obtained a staggering peak weight of 1,400 pounds. *I challenge you to do better.*

❯ "Greatest Weight Loss," Guinness World Records, *www.guinnessworldrecords .com.*

Despite his gargantuan size, Jon Brower Minnoch also holds the record for greatest weight loss. He shed 924 pounds over the course of just sixteen months in 1979. *Lesson: If you want to lose a lot of weight, get really fat first.*

❯ "Greatest Weight Loss," Guinness World Records, *www.guinnessworldrecords .com.*

A lock of Elvis's hair once sold for $115,120. *I'm selling mine for $1.50. So far no takers.*

❯ *National Geographic Kids, Weird But True: 300 Outrageous Facts* (*National Geographic* Children's Books, 2009), 32.

Einstein's Theory of Relativity has gone unchallenged for decades, but many physicists believe Indiana resident Jacob Barnett might be close to unraveling several flaws in the theory. Jacob possesses an IQ of 170; mastered calculus, algebra, and geometry in just two weeks; and can recite pi up to 200 places. He's also twelve. *If he can't figure it out before he discovers masturbation, all hope is lost.*

❯ Michelle Castillo, "12-Year-Old Genius Expands Einstein's Theory of Relativity, Thinks He Can Prove It Wrong," *Time,* March 26, 2011, *www.time.com.*

In 1843, a group of Crow Indians came upon the cabin of John Johnson and killed his wife and unborn child. Upon returning and discovering the scene, Johnson swore an oath to kill every Crow Indian he could find. His savagery was legendary and it is said he killed as many as 300 Crow Indians and ate the liver of each of his victims. *If you are going to go crazy, might as well do it right.*

> George W. Givens, *500 Little-Known Facts in U.S. History* (Cedar Fort, 2006), 165–166.

When she received her General Studies degree from Fort Hays University in 2007, Nola Ochs became the oldest college graduate in history. She was ninety-five at the time. *Is it cheating if you lived through post–industrial American history?*

> "Woman, 95, Set to Be Oldest College Graduate," MSNBC, April 27, 2007, *www.msnbc.msn.com.*

Although not technically a person, a mannequin named "Cynthia" created by Lester Gaba in the 1930s became one of the most famous celebrities of the day. She appeared in several movies, "hosted" her own talk show, and even appeared on the cover of *Life* magazine. *Is it really more strange than idealizing someone for releasing a sex tape?*

> "Cynthia, the World's Most Famous Mannequin," *Life*, May 10, 2011, *www.life.com.*

President John F. Kennedy was capable of reading 2,500 words per minute (about ten times the national average). He could allegedly read six newspapers from cover to cover while eating breakfast. *Which left loads more time for womanizing.*

> "John F. Kennedy," IMDb, *www.imdb.com.*

At eight feet four inches tall, circus performer Al Tomaini towered five feet ten inches above his wife. Also a circus performer, she was born without legs and was only two feet six inches tall. *Legs are overrated anyway. Nobody carries you anywhere.*

> Jami Frater, *The Ultimate Book of Top Ten Lists: A Mind-Boggling Collection of Fun, Fascinating and Bizarre Facts on Movies, Music, Sports, Crime, Celebrities, History, Trivia and More* (Ulysses Press, 2009), 27.

Believing the Catholic church suffered from an overwhelming modernist influence, David Allen Bawden gathered his parents and three other Sedevacantists in Kansas to elect a new pope in 1990. Out of all the millions of potential candidates, the conclave settled on Bawden himself, who took the name Pope Michael I. *Man, what are the odds the new fake pope was right in the room of people choosing the new fake pope?*

> "10 Most Bizarre People on Earth," Oddee, December 6, 2006, *www.oddee.com.*

Donald Rumsfeld is both the youngest and oldest person to serve as Secretary of Defense. He was forty-two when he served under President Ford in 1975 and sixty-eight when he reclaimed the post in 2001. *My brain hurts.*

> "Profile Secretary of Defense Donald Rumsfeld," ABC News, November 1, 2005, *www.abc news.go.com.*

To ensure he always had a clean outfit handy, Apple CEO Steve Jobs kept 100 of his signature black turtlenecks in his closet. *Never trust anyone who owns 100 of anything. Unless it's 100 Medals of Honor. But even then.*

> Dylan Stableford, "Steve Jobs Owned 100 Black Turtlenecks, According to Upcoming Walter Isaacson Biography," Yahoo! News, October 12, 2011, *www.news.yahoo.com.*

In 1849, the Richardson brothers agreed to settle the debt of New York inventor Walter Hunt if he could invent something useful out of a single piece of wire. Three hours later, he invented the safety pin. *Never underestimate a man at the end of his rope.*

> ❯ Ian Harrison, *Take Me to Your Leader* (Dorling Kindersley Ltd., 2007), 314.

Despite the high security at California's San Quentin prison, an inmate in the 1930s managed to avoid the electric chair and end his life on his own terms. By stuffing one of the legs from his cot with playing cards and water and placing it on a heater, inmate William Kogut was able to construct a makeshift bomb that exploded in his cell, killing him instantly. *Not sure I see a downside here.*

> ❯ "The Ingenious Suicide of William Kogut," Science Punk, September 10, 2007, *www.sciencepunk.com.*

After hearing his friends complain about their needy pets in 1975, California ad executive Gary Dahl devised the perfect lazy man's companion—the pet rock. It required no feeding, walking, or care of any kind. Thanks to some clever marketing and a $3.95 price tag the novelty pet made Dahl a millionaire in six months. *He may be richer than you, but at least you'll never be the guy who invented the pet rock.*

> ❯ Tamara Weston, "From Tickle Me Elmo to Squinkies: Top 10 Toy Crazes," December 23, 2010, *Time, www.time.com.*

The pet rock may have made its creator a wealthy man, but they were fairly poor investments for collectors. A mint condition original pet rock sells for only $33 today. *That's about 6 percent interest compounded annually. You could do worse.*

> ❯ Linda Batey, "About Pet Rocks," eHow, *www.ehow.com.*

Although General Washington was originally offered $1,000 per month for his position as head of the colonial army, he nobly declined any payment and instead asked nothing more than that his expenses be paid during the time he held his post. Unfortunately for our fledgling country, by charging things like $6,000 worth of liquor and $800 worth of leather goods, he spent a staggering $449,261.51 during his eight years as general. *He was honest. Not stupid.*

> Jamie Frater, *Listverse.com's Ultimate Book of Bizarre Lists: Fascinating Facts and Shocking Trivia on Movies, Music, Crime, Celebrities, History, and More* (Ulysses Press, 2010), 191.

Washington attempted the same ploy

when he became president, but Congress promptly shut him down and instead awarded him a salary of $25,000 per year. *"Fool me once, shame on . . . shame on you . . . fool me, you can't get fooled again."* —George W. Bush

> Jamie Frater, *Listverse.com's Ultimate Book of Bizarre Lists: Fascinating Facts and Shocking Trivia on Movies, Music, Crime, Celebrities, History, and More* (Ulysses Press, 2010), 191.

Lizzie Velasquez of Austin, Texas, suffers from neonatal progeroid syndrome, a rare disorder that makes it nearly impossible for her to put on weight. To stay alive, she must eat every fifteen to twenty minutes and consumes between 5,000 and 8,000 calories a day. Despite the excessive eating, the five-foot-two-inch woman only weighs fifty-six pounds. *Not sure if I'm envious or sympathetic.*

> David W. Freeman, "Girl Must Eat Every 15 Minutes: Lizzie Velasquez Stays Skeletal Despite Nonstop Eating," CBS News, June 28, 2010, *www.cbsnews.com.*

Bob Weiland lost both legs while fighting in Vietnam, but that didn't stop him from "walking" more than 2,000 miles from California to visit the Vietnam Memorial in Washington, D.C., in 1986. He propelled himself the entire way on his knuckles. *Now don't you feel worthless?*

> "Amazing Military Stories for Memorial Day," Ripley's Believe It or Not!, May 20, 2011, *www.ripleys.com.*

In 1994, seventeen-year-old Eagle Scout David Hahn set out to claim an unofficial scout honor—the nuclear fission badge. Using radioactive materials scavenged from smoke detectors, clocks, gun sights, and other household items, Hahn built a home-made reactor in his mother's tool shed. *The fact that your smoke detector is radioactive is wildly inappropriate.*

> ❯ Ken Silverstein, "The Radio-active Boy Scout," *Harper's Magazine*, November 1998, *www.harpers.org.*

Although it never reached critical mass, David Hahn's dangerous science experiment had to be disposed of by the United States Environmental Protection Agency when it started leaking radiation at 1,000 times normal levels. *Thankfully his experiment eliminated any possibility he might reproduce.*

> ❯ Ken Silverstein, "The Radio-active Boy Scout," *Harper's Magazine*, November 1998, *www.harpers.org.*

Robert Pershing Wadlow of Alton, Illinois, never stopped growing from the day he was born to the day he died. He stood a staggering eight feet eleven inches tall when he died in 1940. *Or 1.6 Smoots.*

> ❯ Jan Payne and Mike Phillips, *The World's Best Book: The Spookiest, Smelliest, Wildest, Oldest, Weirdest, Brainiest, and Funniest Facts* (Running Press Kids, 2009), 13.

Ann Hodges of Sylacauga, Alabama, is the only person to have been directly hit by a meteorite. On November 30, 1954, it crashed into her home and struck her hip while she napped on the couch. *Proof that aliens exist and hate people named Ann Hodges.*

> ❯ Alex Cipriano, "The 7 Most Bizarrely Unlucky People Who Ever Lived," *Cracked*, June 1, 2009, *www.cracked.com.*

The smallest president in history

was James Madison, at five feet four inches tall and ninety-eight pounds. *Or roughly the size of your Great Aunt Miriam.*

❯ Erin Barrett and Jack Mingo, *Random Kinds Of Factness: 1001 (or So) Absolutely True Tidbits About (Mostly) Everything* (Conari Press, 2005), 5.

The famous playwright Tennessee Williams had a habit of unscrewing the lid to his eye drops with his teeth and holding the lid in his mouth while he applied the drops. This ultimately lead to his death, as he accidentally swallowed the lid and choked. *Proof that artistic ability and common sense are inversely related.*

❯ Jamie Frater, *Listverse.com's Ultimate Book of Bizarre Lists: Fascinating Facts and Shocking Trivia on Movies, Music, Crime, Celebrities, History, and More* (Ulysses Press, 2010), 14.

The 1920s silent film star Ben Turpin took out a $20,000 insurance policy in the event his eyes should uncross. *Reread that one all you want, it still won't make sense.*

❯ Ian Harrison, *Take Me to Your Leader* (Dorling Kindersley Ltd., 2007), 148.

Elsie Eiler is the only resident of Monowi, a small town in Nebraska. As the only person living there, she is the town clerk, town treasurer, town secretary, tavern keeper, chief librarian, and mayor. *She is also technically the craziest and most violent person in town. So steer clear.*

❯ Time Reid, "Introducing the Mayor of Monowi: (Population: 1)," *The Sunday Times*, February 19, 2005, *www.timesonline .co.uk.*

Jockey Frank Hayes has the unfortunate honor of being the first and only dead man to win a horse race. He suffered a fatal heart attack in the middle of a race, but his horse "Sweet Kiss" still managed to win. *Shows how useless the jockey is.*

❯ Jamie Frater, *Listverse.com's Ultimate Book of Bizarre Lists: Fascinating Facts and Shocking Trivia on Movies, Music, Crime, Celebrities, History, and More* (Ulysses Press, 2010), 14.

Former vice president Dick Cheney does not have a pulse. In 2010, doctors outfitted him with a device that moves blood through his body, taking much of the burden off of his failing heart. *Sneaky. You can't be charged for war crimes if you're dead.*

❯ Clay Dillow, "Bionic Dick Cheney Technically Has No Pulse," *Popular Science*, July 19, 2010, *www.popsci.com.*

After thirty-seven years as a crayon molder for Crayola and with 1.4 billion crayons under his belt, Emerson Moler revealed when he retired in 1990 that he was colorblind. *So it's his fault I had two burnt siennas and no seafoam blues. Asshole.*

❯ Stacy Conradt, "The Quick 10: 10 Famous Color Blind People," *Mental Floss*, November 9, 2009, *www.mentalfloss.com.*

Before the filming of the film *The Machinist*, actor Christian Bale dropped from a healthy 173 pounds to a skeletal 110 on a diet consisting of a single can of tuna and one apple each day. *So no, you aren't "starving" just because it's been two hours since you last shoved a Dorito in your pie hole.*

> "The Machinist," IMDb, *www.imdb.com.*

Dolly Parton once insured her breasts for $600,000. *Some might call that vain. I'd call it sound financial planning.*

> Ian Harrison, *Take Me to Your Leader* (Dorling Kindersley Ltd., 2007), 148.

With at least twenty-nine confirmed murders under his belt, former nurse Charles Cullen remains America's deadliest serial killer. While working in a New Jersey hospital, Cullen intentionally overdosed his victims with common hospital drugs like insulin and painkillers. He is currently serving eighteen consecutive life sentences. *Somehow, though, he's not the most deplorable thing to come out of Jersey.*

> Charles Graeber, "The Tainted Kidney," *New York* magazine, April 9, 2007, *www.nymag.com.*

Despite popular belief to the contrary, Helen Keller was not born deaf and blind. She was a normal, healthy baby girl until she suffered a serious illness at nineteen months and lost her ability to hear and see. *Sorry, I don't do Helen Keller jokes.*

> "Helen Keller Biography," American Foundation for the Blind, *www.afb.org.*

Salt Lake City native Lee Redmond stopped cutting her fingernails in 1979 at the age of thirty-eight. Twenty-three years and more than twenty-three combined feet of growth later, and she possessed the world's longest fingernails. The most impressive nail, that of her left thumb, measured 31.5 inches. *There are dumber things to be famous for. But not many.*

> Jay Schalder and Eric M. Strauss, "Extreme Measures: The Smallest Waist and the Longest Fingernails," ABC News, November 23, 2007, *www .abcnews.com.*

In 2009, Lee Redmond's famous fingernails shattered when she was ejected from her seat during a car accident. *The driver of the other car deserves a medal.*

> "Lee Redmond, Longest Fingernails Record Holder, Discusses Drama of Breaking Them," *The Huffington Post*, September 3, 2009, *www.huffingtonpost.com.*

Michelle Obama can identify every episode of *The Brady Bunch* simply by viewing the opening shots. *That's still the most useful skill I've heard of a First Lady having.*

> Jodi Kantor, "Teaching Law, Testing Ideas, Obama Stood Slightly Apart," *The New York Times*, July 30, 2008, *www .nytimes.com.*

In 1992, professional gambler Archie Karas drove to Las Vegas with just $50 in his pocket. Six months later, he had grown his bankroll to a staggering $17 million shooting pool and playing poker. During the next three years, Karas would win as much as $40 million before losing it all in a period of just three weeks. *The only way to win in Vegas is to hit up the free buffet and then head straight home.*

> Tom Sexton, "Archie Karas, 'The World's Biggest Gambler,' Part 1," *Poker News*, February 11, 2008, *www.pokernews.com.*

On August 15, 1962, James Joseph Dresnok battled 2.5 miles of landmines to cross the demilitarized zone and defect to North Korea. As of 2011, he has no plans to return and remains the only living American soldier to defect to the country. *The other defectors died from "freedom envy" (read: they starved).*

❯ Mark Russell, "An American in North Korea, Pledging Allegiance to the Great Leader," *The New York Times*, October 19, 2006, *www.nytimes.com.*

Johnny Depp is afraid of clowns. *There are people who aren't?*

❯ Ian Harrison, *Take Me to Your Leader* (Dorling Kindersley Ltd., 2007), 153.

Charlie Chaplin once lost a Charlie Chaplin look-alike contest. *To be fair, the guy who won looked way more like him than him.*

❯ Sidrah Zaheer, "10 Interesting Facts about Charlie Chaplin," Tip Top Tens, *www.tiptoptens.com.*

During divorce proceedings in 1995, Philadelphia lawyer H. Beatty Chadwick claimed he had squandered his $2.75 million fortune and would be unable to provide his soon-to-be-ex-wife with any financial support. The judge didn't buy the story and insisted he pay up or face jail time. He was released fourteen years later without ever paying a dime to his ex. *To my female readers: what a despicable asshole. To my male readers: our hero!*

❯ Jim Avila and Glenn Ruppel, "Lawyer Freed after Longest-Ever Term for Contempt," ABC News, July 17, 2009, *www.abcnews.go.com.*

In 1992, fertility doctor Cecil B. Jacobson was sentenced to five years in prison for impregnating as many as seventy-five of his patients with his own genetic material. The patients believed they were instead receiving sperm from anonymous donors, while at least one patient was under the impression the sperm was that of her husband. *World's most expensive practical joke once they start collecting child support.*

> "Fertility Doctor Gets Five Years," *The New York Times*, May 9, 1992, *www.nytimes.com.*

Victoria's Secret, the company famous for designing women's lingerie, was started by a man, Roy Raymond. *You didn't really think a woman would make you dress like that, did you?*

> "Roy Raymond, 47; Began Victoria's Secret," *The New York Times*, September 2, 1993, *www.nytimes.com.*

John Quincy Adams kept a pet alligator in one of the White House bathrooms.

He reportedly enjoyed watching his guests flee in terror. *Who wouldn't enjoy that?*

> Erin Barrett and Jack Mingo, *Random Kinds Of Factness: 1001 (or So) Absolutely True Tidbits about (Mostly) Everything* (Conari Press, 2005), 3.

Adam West has a small batman logo etched into one of his molars. *You don't want to know where his Robin tattoo is . . .*

> "Adam West," IMDb, *www.imdb.com*

At the age of twenty-one, Frank Abagnale—the notorious con artist featured in the film *Catch Me If You Can*—had scammed about $2.5 million under eight assumed identities in twenty-six countries. He once spent eleven months as a hospital supervisor, despite having no medical training. *You'd be amazed what you can accomplish if you look like you know what you're doing.*

> Ian Harrison, *Take Me to Your Leader* (Dorling Kindersley Ltd., 2007), 106.

Born in 1993, Brooke Greenberg of Reisterstown, Maryland never aged beyond the state of a toddler (both physically and mentally). She is about thirty inches tall and weighs just sixteen pounds. Baffled doctors simply refer to her condition as Syndrome X. *Get to sleep in a crib forever, people feed you and change your diapers . . . I don't see the problem.*

> Bob Brown, "Doctors Baffled, Intrigued by Girl Who Doesn't Age," ABC News, June 23, 2009, *www.abcnews.go.com.*

CHAPTER 10

Happy National Crown Roast of Pork Day!
Eccentric American Holidays and Festivals to Enjoy

If there's something worth celebrating, you can guarantee that somewhere in America there is a festival or holiday in its honor. And if something isn't worth celebrating, well there's plenty of Americans willing to hold a parade all the same. From Bubble Wrap Appreciation Day to an entire festival devoted to the humble mosquito, America has it covered.

So if you're looking for a reason to take the day off from work, or you just want an excuse to eat some cake, you are sure to find plenty of wacky holidays here to get you started.

In 1980, President Jimmy Carter officially changed the name of "Senior Citizens Month"—celebrated in May to honor Americans over the age of sixty-five—to "Older Americans Month." Nearly 40 million Americans currently fall into this category, but that number is expected to surpass 88 million by 2050. *A month of acknowledgment pales in comparison to half-priced movie tickets and a free pass to complain about everything.*

❭ "Older Americans Month: May 2011," United States Census Bureau, *www.census.gov.*

The annual music festival Lollapalooza shares its name with a word American soldiers employed to identify spies during World War II. If a suspect could not pronounce the word correctly, they assumed he was not American. *A nice catch-all if you want an excuse to kill somebody.*

❭ "Lollapalooza Tickets," StubHub, *www.stubhub.com.*

In July 2012, UFO enthusiasts from around the world gathered in Roswell, New Mexico, to celebrate the sixty-fifth anniversary of the alleged crash landing of an alien spacecraft in 1947. Dubbed "The Amazing Roswell UFO Festival," the annual event includes lectures, parades, an alien costume contest, and other supernaturally themed events. *Alleged my ass.*

❭ J. A. Getzlaff, "Mike the Headless Chicken Day," *Salon,* January 6, 2007, *www.salon.com.*

Each year, Americans erect between 30 and 35 million Christmas trees in their homes. *Also, the number of presents you receive directly correlates to how much your family loves you.*

❭ "Christmas," History Channel, *www.history.com.*

To commemorate the birthday of John Montagu, the Fourth Earl of Sandwich credited with inventing the snack that shares his name, the United States celebrates National Sandwich Day on November 3. *America: Where no accomplishment is too inane to deserve its own day.*

❯ "National Sandwich Day: Name the Best Sandwich Filling," *The Guardian*, November 3, 2011, *www.guardian.co.uk.*

National Mustard Day falls each year on the first Saturday in August. *And there is much rejoicing.*

❯Deanna Hyland, "9 Unusual Food Museums That Amuse and Educate," *BootsnAll*, November 16, 2009, *www.bootsnall.com.*

On October 9, cheese aficionados and fungus enthusiasts unite for the annual celebration of Moldy Cheese Day. *Are we celebrating blue cheese, or is this an excuse to throw out that fuzzy lump of mold that used to be cheese in the fridge?*

❯ The Ultimate Holiday Site, Hallmark, *www.theultimate holidaysite.com.*

Each May the citizens of Fruita, Colorado, celebrate "Mike the Headless Chicken Day," in honor of Miracle Mike, a rooster turned sideshow attraction who survived for eighteen months after his head was chopped off in 1945. *Apparently there isn't much going on in Colorado.*

❯ J. A. Getzlaff, "Mike the Headless Chicken Day," *Salon*, January 6, 2007, *www.salon .com.*

The Portland Pirate Festival earned the record for "most pirates gathered in one place" in 2009 when 1,670 participants arrived dressed as pirates for the event. The record was surpassed during England's Brixham Pirate Festival the following year. *Arrrgggg! Scallywags! Shiver me timbers! And other pirate clichés!!!*

> Kari Bodnarchuk, "Weird Meets Wild at Annual Festivals," *The Boston Globe*, www.boston.com.

Although not wildly celebrated, Pet Owners' Independence Day is a holiday that encourages animal lovers to take the day off and send their furry friends into the office in their stead. *Bad move. What if he does a better job?*

> Denice Skrepcinski and Lois Lyles, *Silly Celebrations!: Activities for the Strangest Holidays You've Never Heard Of* (Aladdin, 1998), 29.

The last Monday of January is national "Bubble Wrap Appreciation Day," to mark the anniversary of the ubiquitous packing material's invention. *But really, you should appreciate it year round.*

> "Bubble Wrap Appreciation Day 2010: What It Is, How to Celebrate Bubble Wrap, Sealed Air Product," *The Huffington Post*, January 25, 2010, www.huffingtonpost.com.

The Maine Lobster Fest culminates with the Great International William Atwood Lobster Crate Race, which takes place on the final day. Contestants run back and forth across a bridge of fifty partially submerged lobster crates as many times as possible before falling into the ocean. The current record is 4,501 crates by twelve-year-old Andrew Bachiochi of Connecticut. *Well, Andy, you've peaked. It's all downhill from here.*

> Chris Clark, "7 Classic and/or Weird American Summer Food Festivals," *BootsnAll*, June 4, 2009, www.bootsnall.com.

Submissions to the Marshall, Texas, Fire Ant Festival chili cook-off must contain at least one fire ant. *Do the world a favor and make sure they are alive when you put them in. It's not cruel if it's revenge.*

> Kari Bodnarchuk, "Weird Meets Wild at Annual Festivals," *The Boston Globe, www.boston.com.*

Although St. Patrick's Day—which falls on March 17—is not a national holiday, Boston residents discovered a loophole in 1941. Then-governor Leverett Saltonstall declared that date to be "Evacuation Day" in honor of the day the British left Boston in 1776. *God bless those lovable drunks.*

> Dave Shaw and Kevin McNicholas, "With a Signature in Green, St. Patrick's Day Became a Holiday," NPR, May 12, 2010, *www.wbur.org.*

Operation T-Bone is an event that takes place each summer in Iowa to honor the days when local cattle would board trains to Chicago stockyards. *Goodbye old friends. You go now to a better place. Well, not really better . . . just different.*

> "12 Strange Tourist Attractions," How Stuff Works, *www.tlc.howstuffworks.com.*

Aside from Halloween, the evening of October 31 heralds the beginning of Movember, a holiday devoted to facial hair. Participants shave their faces and refrain from shaving again until the end of November to raise money and awareness for prostate cancer. *How exactly does not shaving = ending prostate cancer?*

❯ Maura Judkis, "No Shave November, or Movember: the Art of the Moustache," *The Washington Post*, November 1, 2011, *www.washingtonpost .com.*

Each year on August 10, children and adults around the country celebrate S'more Day by indulging in the time-honored combination of graham crackers, chocolate, and marshmallows. *I call it "National Watch* Sandlot *and Laugh At That One Part Where They Make S'mores Day."*

❯ Ann Nungesser, "Go Gourmet for S'more Day," About. com, August 10, 2011, *www.neworleans.about.com.*

After the combined stress of Thanksgiving, Christmas, and New Year's Eve, many Americans spend January 3 celebrating Festival of Sleep Day where participants are encouraged to spend the entire day in bed. *AKA Sunday.*

❯ "Festival of Sleep Day," Holiday Insights, *www.holidayinsights.com.*

September 27 is national
Crush a Can Day.
I didn't feel that one required an explanation.

❯ Pam Gaulin, "Sept. 27: Crush a Can Day, Corned Beef Hash Day, Ancestor Appreciation Day, Perigean Spring Tides," Yahoo! News, September 12, 2011, *www.news.yahoo.com.*

Gilroy, California, is one of the largest producers of garlic in the world, so it's no surprise they host an entire festival devoted to the popular ingredient. The festival features everything from typical favorites like garlic bread to more adventurous fare like garlic ice cream. *I like garlic, I like ice cream . . . I don't see a problem here.*

› Chris Clark, "7 Classic and/or Weird American Summer Food Festivals," *BootsnAll*, June 4, 2009, *www.bootsnall.com.*

During the first Friday of June Americans celebrate National Doughnut Day to honor Salvation Army volunteers who distributed doughnuts to soldiers on the front line during World War I. *I'm fighting the "war against ignorance of obscure holidays" here. Where's my treat?*

› Kevin Fagan, "A Holey Holiday-National Doughnut Day," *San Francisco Chronicle*, June 6, 2009, *www.sfgate.com.*

The World Water Tasting Competition takes place each year in Berkeley Springs, West Virginia. A panel of judges tastes and rates nearly 100 samples of water from eight countries to determine the highest quality H_2O available. *I miss the days where you could drink water from a hose without being judged.*

› "Weird Festival Photos: Snake Roundups, Worm Races, More," *National Geographic*, *www .news.nationalgeographic.com.*

Pauls Valley, Oklahoma, is home to the annual Okie Noodling Tournament, a day-long race to bag the largest catfish using nothing but the contestants' bare hands. *I've seen some of the fish, and honestly, I think they could take me.*

› "Big Mouth," *National Geographic*, *www.travel.nationalgeographic.com.*

The first 500 people who arrive at Avon, Ohio's annual Duct Tape Festival receive a free roll of the ubiquitous DIY tool. *If duct tape doesn't fix it, try WD-40. If that doesn't work, give up.*

❯ "Retro Rewind: Peace, Love and . . . Duck Tape®!," Duck Tape, *www.duckbrand.com.*

In 2009 the Center For Inquiry declared September 30 to be Blasphemy Day, a holiday devoted to expressing criticisms about religion and questioning established dogma. *If God can't forgive blasphemy, just imagine how he's going to react to that whole incident with the gerbil and the microwave.*

❯ Moni Basu, "Taking Aim at God on 'Blasphemy Day,'" CNN, September 30, 2009, *www.cnn.com.*

On April 1, 1996, Taco Bell ran an ad in *The New York Times* announcing they had purchased the Liberty Bell and renamed it the Taco Liberty Bell. Thousands of citizens called to complain before they realized it was an April Fools' Day joke. *If Taco Bell had turned it upside down and filled it with nacho cheese, people would have supported the change.*

❯ "Top 10 Successful Marketing Stunts," *Entrepreneur*, May 27, 2010, *www.entrepreneur.com.*

The National Christmas Tree can be found in California's Sequoia National Park. Named "General Grant," the nearly 270-foot sequoia is more than 1,700 years old. *If we cut it up, we could easily convert it into 10,000 normal-sized ones. Just saying.*

❯ "General Grant, Nation's Christmas Tree," See California, *www.seecalifornia.com.*

Each year, thousands of Arizona State University students strip down to their knickers for the ASU Undie Run Festival. Clothes removed by the student body during the event are later donated to various charities around the state. *If you miss the event, just hang around the dorms on any Friday night and be patient. You will see someone in their underwear.*

> "History," ASU Undie Run, *www.asuundierun.com.*

The highlight of the annual Potato Day Festival held in Barnesville, Minnesota, is the mashed potato wrestling ring. It's one of the few places on earth where combatants can settle their differences in a thick potato goo before being hosed off by the local fire department. *Is there anything mashed potatoes can't do?*

> Kari Bodnarchuk, "Weird Meets Wild at Annual Festivals," *The Boston Globe, www.boston.com.*

On October 23 between the hours of 6:02 A.M. and 6:02 P.M. nerds around the country unite in celebration of the mole, a unit of measure used in chemistry. *It unironically corresponds with national celibacy day.*

> Anne Marie Helmenstine, PhD, "What Mole Day Is, When Mole Day Is, and How To Celebrate Mole Day," About.com, *www.chemistry.about.com.*

Each August, thousands of LEGO enthusiasts gather in Northern Virginia for the annual Brick-Fair event. The group is sponsored by the Adult Fans of LEGO group who offer LEGO building workshops alongside LEGO robot sumo wrestling, stop-motion animated LEGO films, and LEGO bingo. *It's like being a kid, but with enough self awareness to realize how lame you are.*

❯ Kari Bodnarchuk, "Weird Meets Wild at Annual Festivals," *The Boston Globe*, www.boston.com.

Part monster truck rally, part demolition derby, the School Bus Figure 8 Races in Bithlo, Florida, are a car-nage enthusiast's dream. Several school buses run on a figure-8 course and try to avoid colliding with one another (which happens a lot) or tipping over (which is almost inevitable). Some drivers ride in ordinary yellow school buses, while others have their own custom racing buses built specifically for the event. *Judge all you want, but you'd totally cheer if you were there.*

❯ "Bithlo, Florida—School Bus Figure 8 Races," *Roadside America*, www.roadsideamerica.com.

March is national
Frozen Food Month.

Just kidding. Every month is national Frozen Food Month.

❯ "Everday Mysteries," Library of Congress, *www.loc.gov*.

Although initially a joke on the hit sitcom *Seinfeld*, the holiday of "Festivus" is now a very real tradition for many fans. Each December 23, followers erect an aluminum Festivus pole and berate their family members in a ceremonial "airing of grievances." The celebration does not conclude until the head of the family has been wrestled to the ground in the annual "feats of strength" competition. *Just like Christmas, but with 50 percent more tears.*

❯ Allen Alkin, "Fooey To the World: Festivus Is Come," *The New York Times*, December 19, 2004, *www.nytimes.com*.

October 6 is proudly celebrated in the United States as Mad Hatter Day, where citizens are encouraged to embrace silliness and act in a manner opposite to usual decorum. The holiday is so named because in one of the original illustrations for *Alice in Wonderland* a slip of paper reading "In this style 10/6" adorned the the Mad Hatter's hat. *Just remember, explain the holiday to people before you slap them in the face with a raw chicken. Not after.*

> Katrina Rossos, "Five Things to Know Today: Oct. 6, 2011, Mad Hatter Day," *Manalapan Patch*, October 6, 2011, *www.manalapan.patch.com.*

On December 25, 1984, a group of anti-abortionists bombed three abortion clinics in Pensacola, Florida. Members of the group later claimed the act was meant as a "gift to Jesus on his birthday." *Looks like somebody snuck a peek at our little savior's letter to Santa.*

> Associated Press, "Abortion Clinic Bombings Meant as 'Gift to Jesus'," *Los Angeles Times*, January 4, 1985, *www.latimes .com.*

Started in 1958, the World's Largest Rattlesnake Round-Up takes place each year in Sweetwater, Texas, during the second weekend of March. Guests can go on a guided rattlesnake hunt, receive rattlesnake handling lessons, and watch professional wranglers round up thousands of snakes. *Never. Not even if I had cancer and the only cure was watching idiots get bitten by rattlesnakes.*

> Elizabeth R. Rose, "Rattlesnake Roundup—Sweetwater, Texas," About.com, *www.gosw .about.com.*

Each year, the annual rattlesnake round-up in Sweetwater, Texas, eliminates approximately 1 percent of the state's rattlesnake population. *Come on, guys, you can do better than that.*

> Associated Press, "Texas Town Welcomes Rattlesnakes, Handlers," Fox News, March 15, 2006, *www.foxnews.com.*

In 1998, Michael Cameron of Evans, Georgia, was suspended for one day for wearing a Pepsi shirt on Coke in Education Day. *Monster.*

❯ "The Media Business: A Pepsi Fan Is Punished in Coke's Backyard," *The New York Times*, March 26, 1998, *www.nytimes.com.*

In honor of National Donut Day, Dunkin' Donuts launched the company's first Create Dunkin's Next Donut contest on June 3, 2010. Donut enthusiast Rachel Davis won with her Monkey-See, Monkey-Donut confection that sports a Bananas Foster filling, chocolate frosting, and Reese's Peanut Butter shavings. *My Tur-donut—a bear claw stuffed with a French cruller, stuffed with a jelly donut, stuffed with a munchkin—was deemed too dangerous for public consumption.*

❯ Todd Wasserman, "National Donut Day Sparks Twitter Trivia Contest," Mashable, June 3, 2011, *www.mashable.com.*

October 5 is the most popular birthday date in the United States. *Nine months and five days after New Year's Eve, for those of you scoring at home.*

❯ Celebrate October 5: America's Most Popular Birthday! 1-800 Flowers, *www.1800flowers.com.*

Eighty-eight percent of Americans consume turkey on Thanksgiving, resulting in the consumption of 46 million birds in a single day. *Nothing is more delicious than excess. Except possibly gravy.*

❯ "Thanksgiving Facts," History Channel, *www.history.com.*

When the residents of Whalan, Minnesota (population: sixty-two), wanted to have a parade in 1995, they didn't let the small size of their town stop them. They simply set up the band, floats, fire engines, and color guard on the main street and let the spectators move around the stationary parade. The Stand Still Parade was such a success they have staged one each year since. *Odd, we are generally too lazy for this kind of thing to catch on.*

❭ "The Sixteenth Annual Stand Still Parade," Whalan, Minnesota's Annual Stand Still Parade, *www.standstillparade.org.*

Each year, groups of outhouse enthusiasts brave the Anchorage, Alaska, winter for the annual Anchorage Outhouse Races. Participants attach commodes of all shapes and sizes to skis and race for the fastest time on a downhill trail. *Pushing is fine, but never drive. Don't ask why.*

❭ "Discover How Fast an Outhouse Can Move, and Match Speeds with Reindeer at Fur Rendezvous," Anchorage Convention & Visitors Bureau, February 1, 2010, *www.anchorage.net.*

The third week in September is National Unmarried and Single Americans Week. *Remember, if you surround yourself with enough cats, you're never truly alone.*

❭ "History," Unmarried America, *www.unmarriedamerica.org.*

March 7 is National Crown Roast of Pork Day, a day set aside for the cooking and consumption of a very specific cut of pork. The holiday is not officially acknowledged by Congress. *Representatives of the people, my ass.*

❭ "National Crown Roast of Pork Day," Holiday Insights, *www.holidayinsights.com.*

According to Groundhog Day lore, the groundhog named Punxsutawney Phil who predicts the weather each February 2 in Pennsylvania has been on the job for more than a century. He gets his longevity from drinking "groundhog punch" each summer, an elixir that increases his lifespan by seven years. *I see no holes in that logic whatsoever.*

❯ "Frequently Asked Questions about Groundhog Day," Punxsutawney Groundhog Club, *www.groundhog.org.*

Groundhogese is the official language of Punxsutawney Phil. The Groundhog Club President supposedly translates his prediction into vernacular before sharing it with the rest of the world. *Just remember, people far smarter than you have believed things much dumber than this throughout history.*

❯ "Frequently Asked Questions about Groundhog Day," Punxsutawney Groundhog Club, *www.groundhog.org.*

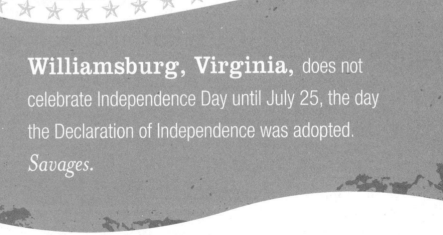

Williamsburg, Virginia, does not celebrate Independence Day until July 25, the day the Declaration of Independence was adopted. *Savages.*

❯ Tim O'Brian, "Let Freedom (and Strange July 4th Facts) Ring! Ripley's Believe It or Not! Chronicles Independence Day Oddities, Such as When the Liberty Bell 'Really' Rang For the First Time!," *Ripley's Newsroom,* June 13, 2011, *www.ripleysnewsroom.com.*

While it's true none of the characters in A. A. Milne's Winnie the Pooh stories ever made much of a fuss over Eeyore, he's a star among residents of Austin, Texas. Each year, they stage a party for the disgruntled donkey on the final Saturday in April. *Seriously, Pooh, you have like five friends. How hard is it to remember?*

❯ Joshunda Sanders, "Eeyore's 47th Birthday Party," *Austin American-Statesman*, April 24, 2010, *www.statesman.com.*

National Smile Week was not created to endorse having an upbeat attitude, but instead to promote good oral hygiene. *So by all means smile, but only if you're not ugly.*

❯ "Put on a Happy Face, It's National Smile Week," CBS News, August 11, 2010, *www.newyork.cbslocal.com.*

The great Texas Mosquito Festival attracts some 15,000 visitors each year. Events include a mosquito-calling contest, haystack dive, and a baby crawling contest, all under the careful watch of the festival's mascot Willie Man-Chew, a twenty-six-foot inflatable yellow mosquito sporting a cowboy hat. *So the losing babies get bitten by mosquitoes?*

❯ Kari Bodnarchuk, "Weird Meets Wild at Annual Festivals," *The Boston Globe*, *www.boston.com.*

Mall Santas generally earn between $100 and $200 per hour during the holiday season. Those willing to work on Christmas Eve and Christmas Day can earn as much as $300 an hour. *So yes, even the alcoholic in the fake beard earns more than you.*

❯ Erin Joyce, "Santa's Salary: the Highest Paid Holiday Help," *Financial Edge*, December 23, 2010, *www.financialedge.investopedia.com.*

Each year, citizens of Delmarva, the region where Delaware, Maryland, and Virginia come together, cook nearly three tons of chicken at the Delmarva Chicken Festival, an event devoted to raising awareness of the region and celebrating its thriving chicken industry. *Since this is probably the first time you have heard the word "Delmarva," I'd say the event isn't working.*

❯ "62nd Delmarva Chicken Festival Ends," WGMD, June 19, 2011, *www.wgmd.com.*

The majority of the chicken at the Delmarva Chicken Festival is cooked in the world's largest frying pan, which has a diameter of ten feet and weighs 650 pounds. *I can't decide of that's dumb or awesome. But either way I want to see it.*

❯ "62nd Delmarva Chicken Festival Ends," WGMD, June 19, 2011, *www.wgmd.com.*

In 2009, Congress approved a resolution designating March 14 as "National Pi Day," and encouraging schools to use the holiday to teach students about pi and to appreciate mathematics. *Sounds irrational. Also, consider yourself lucky if you don't get that joke.*

❯ Declan McCullagh, "National Pi Day? Congress Makes It Official," CNet, March 11, 2009, *www.news.cnet.com.*

September 16 is an opportunity for citizens to reclaim the nation's metered parking spaces and transform them into temporary play areas. Observers of "Parking Day," started in San Francisco in 2005, max out the meter and use the time to play catch, lounge in chairs, and decorate the space however they see fit. *Stick it to the Man by putting money in the meter. That'll show them.*

❯ Sarah Goodyear, "Park(ing) Day 2010 Liberates Parking Spots for Human Use," *The Grist*, September 17, 2010, *www.grist.org.*

To replace its controversial rattlesnake roundup, residents of Fitzgerald, Georgia, decided instead to honor its population of wild Burmese chickens. The Wild Chicken Festival attracts about 10,000 visitors each March and culminates in a massive chicken dance. *Such is the plight of the chicken: Humans would rather kill them than harm poisonous snakes.*

> "Fitzgerald Wild Chicken Festival," Animal Tourism.com, *www.animaltourism.com.*

More than 600 individuals were arrested in Washington, D.C., during the 1975 Human Kindness Day. The event drew a crowd of 125,000 individuals who committed 500 robberies, thirty-two acts of arson, and seventeen acts of violence toward police officers. *The organizers assumed humans are inherently decent. That's adorable.*

> Leland Gregory, *Stupid History: Tales of Stupidity, Strangeness, and Mythconceptions Throughout the Ages* (Andrews McMeel, 2007), 36.

Christmas was officially outlawed in colonial Boston from 1659 to 1681. The punishment for celebrating the holiday was five shillings. *The Pilgrims hated fun.*

> "Christmas," History Channel, *www.history.com.*

The annual Burning Man Festival held in Nevada has a temporary airport, a post office, two daily newspapers, a recycling center, and a pizza delivery service that all exist only during the event. *Let's not forget the patchouli manufacturing plant.*

> "Burning Man 101: Fast Facts about the Event," *San Francisco Chronicle*, March 29, 2005, *www.sfgate.com.*

In Spivey's Corner, North Carolina, there is an annual contest devoted to the lost art of "Hollerin'" (an archaic means of communication not to be confused with cat-calling). Participants in the Hollerin' Contest take to the stage—for no more than four minutes—and compete to see whose loud hoots and shouts can carry the farthest. *They'll give prizes for anything these days.*

❯ Willy Volk, "10 Weird Summer Festivals," *Gadling*, May 3, 2007, *www.gadling.com.*

Every March 20, legions of intrepid alien hunters gather to celebrate "Alien Abduction Day." Participants trade abduction stories and keep their eyes on the sky in the hopes of a close encounter. *They're not crazy. Just sad.*

❯ "Alien Abduction Day Arrives, but Will Little Green Men?" Fox News, March 20, 2010, *www.foxnews.com.*

During the annual Yellow Pine Harmonica Contest and Festival, the population of Yellow Pine, Idaho, explodes from just forty individuals to more than 3,500. *To put it in perspective, imagine living with one roommate on Tuesday and having to deal with 87.5 roommates on Wednesday.*

❯ Kari Bodnarchuk, "Weird Meets Wild at Annual Festivals," *The Boston Globe*, *www.boston.com.*

Coinciding with Labor Day, the Wisconsin State Chip Throw finds contestants competing to see who can pitch a patty of dried cow dung the farthest. Participants are not permitted to wear gloves. *Two tickets please.*

❯ J. A. Getzlaff, "Mike the Headless Chicken Day," *Salon*, January 6, 2007, *www.salon.com.*

Ocean City, New Jersey, is home to the annual Quiet Festival, an event where participants come together to appreciate the joy of silence. Gatherers are known to throw leaves into the air and watch them fall, compete in "yawn-offs," and indulge in group naps. *Well guys, you know what we must do. I'll grab my Vuvuzela.*

> "Weird Festival Photos: Snake Roundups, Worm Races, More," *National Geographic,* www .news.nationalgeographic.com.

Each year, a group of pumpkin enthusiasts gather in Damariscotta, Maine, for the annual Damariscotta Pumpkin Fest and Regatta. Aside from the typical carved gourds one might expect at such a celebration, visitors can watch as contestants race giant pumpkin boats outfitted with outboard motors. *What could possibly go wrong?*

> John Maguire, "Damariscotta Pumpkin Festival and Regatta Set to Begin," *The Coastal Journal,* September 22, 2011, www.coastaljournal.com.

Plumbers receive 50 percent more calls the day after Thanksgiving than they do on any other Friday throughout the year. *What goes in, must come out.*

> Lisa Ermak, "Day after Thanksgiving a Boon for Plumbers," *The Holland Sentinel,* November 24, 2011, www.hollandsentinel.com.

> "Wear Your Pajamas to Work," NPR, April 18, 2006, www.npr.org.

Each year on April 18, hordes of lazy Americans skip their usual morning routine in celebration of "Wear Your Pajamas to Work Day." Sadly, the holiday is not nationally recognized, and not all employers allow workers to participate. *When you work from home, every day is Wear Your Pajamas to Work Day. It's not as fun as it sounds.*

The Annual Frozen Dead Guys Days take place each March in Nederland, Colorado, to honor the eccentric Trygve Bauge who kept the bodies of his deceased grandfather and cryogenics enthusiast Al Campbell frozen in his backyard shed. *Writing this book has poisoned my mind. I don't really think this is weird anymore.*

❯ Bill Geist, *Way Off the Road* (Broadway Books, 2007), 36–39.

You must be twenty-one or older to participate in Clinton, Montana's "Testicle Festival," a celebration of the Rocky Mountain Oyster (a.k.a. deep-fried bull testicles). *You are really never old enough to eat bull balls.*

❯ J. A. Getzlaff, "Mike the Headless Chicken Day," *Salon*, January 6, 2007, *www.salon .com*.

The first "Redneck Games" were founded by Mac Davis in 1996 as a rebuttal to the Atlanta Olympics. The events take place each year in Georgia and include the Mudpit Belly Flop, Hubcap Hurl, the Armpit Serenade, and Bobbin' For Pigs' Feet. *You must be this smart to attend. (You can't see, but I'm holding my hand very low to the ground.)*

❯ Ian Harrison, *Take Me to Your Leader* (Dorling Kindersley Ltd., 2007), 322.

CHAPTER 11

From the Salem Witch Trials to Saddam Hussein's Secret Sex Tape

Strange Moments in American History to Dumbfound

If you think the general air of weirdness wafting around this country is a new development, think again. Our forefathers were exponentially stranger than we could ever hope to be, and I've got the facts to prove it.

From the first American to take a leak on the moon to the live nuclear missile that the military "misplaced" in the 1950s, here's a catalog of our history's strangest missteps for you to relive and enjoy. After all, education is the first step toward making sure we don't nominate Hitler again as *Time*'s Man of the Year.

Shortly after the attack on Pearl Harbor, the Secret Service found itself scrambling to procure a bulletproof limousine to protect the president. They eventually settled on an armored 1928 Cadillac 341A Town Sedan that had been seized years earlier from none other than Al Capone. *"Let's use this old mob car. What could possibly go wrong?"*

> "President Roosevelt Used to Ride Around in Al Capone's Limousine," The Forgotten History Blog, *www.history.verdeserve .com.*

In 1909, members of Yale's mysterious Skull and Bones secret society traveled to the grave of Geronimo and allegedly returned home with a souvenir— the Apache leader's skull. Since then, the group insists they do not know the skull's whereabouts, but many claim the relic plays an integral part in the society's initiation rights. *"Oh, that skull? That was there when we moved in."*

> Ishaan Tharoor, "Top 10 Famous Stolen Body Parts," *Time*, May 12, 2010. *www .time.com.*

One of the goals of the Lewis and Clark expedition was to determine if mastodons were still alive. *And enslave them. Naturally.*

> Elin Woodger, Brandon Toropov, and Ned Blackhawk, *Encyclopedia of the Lewis and Clark Expedition* (Facts on File, 2003), 373.

During the Vietnam War, imprisoned naval pilot Jeremiah Denton was forced to conduct a propaganda interview for a Hanoi television station. Realizing he could use the cameras to send a message to the U.S. government, Denton managed to convey the word "torture" by blinking his eyes in Morse code. *"Please send guns," might have been more helpful.*

> Alan Bellows, *Alien Hand Syndrome and Other Too-Weird-to-Be-True Stories* (Workman Publishing, 2009), 275.

During his presidency,

John Quincy Adams approved an expedition to travel to the center of the earth via the North Pole to prove that the planet was actually hollow. *Cocaine's a hell of a drug.*

❯ Ethan Lou, "6 Presidential Secrets Your History Teacher Didn't Mention," *Cracked*, January 4, 2011, *www.cracked.com.*

The FBI was founded by Charles Joseph Bonaparte, attorney general to Theodore Roosevelt and the grandnephew of Napoleon Bonaparte. *Always beware of the long con.*

❯ "Historical Documents from the Bureau's Founding," Federal Bureau of Investigation," *www.fbi.gov.*

Components of the bomb that America dropped on Hiroshima on August 6, 1945, left San Francisco just four hours after the first successful atomic bomb test occurred in New Mexico on July 16 for Tinian Island in the Western Pacific. *Always best to rush a decision like that. Less chance you'll second-guess yourself and do the "right" thing.*

❯ William S. Kowinski, "Hiroshima: The Birth of Nuclear Warfare/How the U.S. Got to Dr. Strangelove/Nuclear Weapons Changed the World," *San Francisco Chronicle*, July 31, 2005, *www.sfgate.com.*

Amish men do not start to grow their beards until after they marry. They do shave the area above their lips, because they shun the military and do not wish not to emulate nineteenth-century generals who wore both beards and mustaches.
And then there's that whole Hitler thing . . .

❯ "The Amish," BBC, www.bbc.co.uk.

During the Civil War, Frank C. Armstrong was the only general officer to fight on both sides, as a captain for the Union army and a brigadier for the Confederacy.
Any decision is better than indecision.

❯ Webb Garrison, *Civil War Trivia and Fact Book: Unusual and Often Overlooked Facts About America's Civil War* (Thomas Nelson, 1992), 12.

Only 13 percent of Americans believe Lee Harvey Oswald acted alone in the assassination of President John F. Kennedy. *Apparently only a few of us are as dumb as I thought.*

❯ Ian Harrison, *Take Me to Your Leader* (Dorling Kindersley Ltd., 2007), 91.

In 1947, the sitcom *Mary Kay and Johnny* became the first American show to depict a married couple sleeping in the same bed. Despite that fact, many later sitcoms—like the popular show *I Love Lucy*—implied the main characters slept in separate beds. *Apparently they pooped out the window, because I'll be damned if I saw a bathroom before 1980.*

❯ "Early to Bed," Snopes, www.snopes.com.

By most accounts, Abraham Lincoln possessed a high, shrill voice, in contrast to the deep baritone he is portrayed with in films. *But . . . but . . . why would Hollywood lie to us?*

> Megan Gambino, "Ask an Expert: What Did Abraham Lincoln's Voice Sound Like?" *Smithsonian* magazine, June 7, 2011, *www.smithsonianmag.com.*

The original copy of the Constitution is kept in the National Archives Building in Washington, D.C., where several pages are displayed during the day behind a bulletproof case filled with helium and water vapor to preserve it. At night, the pages are stored in a vault with a five-ton door designed to withstand a nuclear explosion. *Could explain why the government forgets so often what's written there.*

> Terry L. Jordan, *The U.S. Constitution: And Fascinating Facts About It* (Oak Hill Publishing Co., 1999), 25.

The original draft of the Constitution spells the Keystone State's name "Pensylvania."
Close enough.

> Terry L. Jordan, *The U.S. Constitution: And Fascinating Facts About It* (Oak Hill Publishing Co., 1999), 25.

So far, no American president has

been an only child. *Do we really want somebody running the country who never learned to share?*

❯ Erin Barrett and Jack Mingo, *Random Kinds Of Factness: 1001 (or So) Absolutely True Tidbits About (Mostly) Everything* (Conari Press, 2005), 3.

Throughout history, there have been at least eighteen assassination attempts on sitting U.S. presidents, four of which succeeded. *Does the guy who threw a shoe at George W. Bush count?*

❯ A. P. Holiday, *Hmm . . . I Did Not Know That* (Haymaker Book Company, 2011).

The Pilgrims brought **more beer than water** on the *Mayflower*.

Don't act like you're surprised.

❯ "Great Western Malting Company," History Link, *www.historylink.org*.

In 1999, the United States government paid the family of Abraham Zapruder, the man who recorded the famous JFK assassination video, $16 million for the film. *Don't be fooled though, 99.999 percent of home videos are still worthless.*

❯ Ethan Trex, "5 Things You Didn't Know About Abraham Zapruder," Mental Floss, *www.mentalfloss.com*.

As of 2011, former president John Tyler still has two living grandchildren. Tyler was the tenth president and was born in 1790. *Don't even try to do the math. It hurts.*

❯ Adam Goodheart, "The Ashen Ruin," *The New York Times*, February 15, 2011, *www.nytimes.com.*

According to documents obtained by journalist Hank Albarelli, an event of mass hysteria that occurred in Pont-Saint-Esprit, France, in 1951 could have been caused by the CIA. Albarelli alleges that, in order to test the possibility of using LSD as a weapon, the government agency slipped the drug into the bread of a popular baker. The resulting hallucinations caused one man to jump from a hospital window, believing himself to be a dragonfly. *Drugs are always best enjoyed at ground level.*

❯Christophe Schpoliansky, "Did CIA Experiment LSD on French Town?" ABC News, March 23, 2010, *www.abcnews.go.com.*

The USS *Iowa* is the only naval ship built with a bathtub, at the behest of President Roosevelt. *Essential for planning attacks with plastic boats and rubber duckies.*

❯ "USS Iowa Facts," Save the Iowa, *www.savetheiowa.com.*

To prove Americans would read anything as long as there was enough sex in it, *Newsday* columnist Mike McGrady gathered a team of twenty-four writers in 1966 to produce the most insipid, sex-soaked romance novel in history. The resulting work, *Naked Came the Stranger*, became a runaway bestseller and inspired a host of copycat collaborations.
Every time you read a romance novel, an English major dies.

❯ "Naked Came the Stranger," Museum of Hoaxes, *www.museumofhoaxes.com.*

Until 1977, the launch code for the U.S. nuclear arsenal was 00,00,00,00,00,00. *Further evidence that the government is run by your five-year-old sister.*

❯ Ruben Roel, "Launch Code for the US Nuclear Arsenal Was All Zeroes Until 1977," Tek-Bull, June 29, 2011, *www.tek-bull.com.*

The year 1816 is commonly known as "The Year Without Summer." Its unusual weather was most likely due to a volcanic eruption in the Pacific Ocean the previous year. Connecticut experienced a blizzard in June, and high temperatures in Georgia dropped to the forties in July. *Global warming doesn't seem so bad now, does it?*

❯ Phyllis Goldman, *Monkeyshines on Strange and Wonderful Facts* (Monkeyshines, 1991), 9.

When **Elvis Presley** died on August 16, 1977, he had consumed at least fourteen different prescription drugs. *Go big or go home.*

❯ Ian Harrison, *Take Me to Your Leader* (Dorling Kindersley Ltd., 2007), 331.

When the first operating phone service was established in 1878, the formal greeting was "Ahoy," instead of "Hello." *God bless our pirate ancestors.*

❯ "The Discovernator," Discovery Channel, *www.news.discovery.com.*

It is a common myth that accused witches were burned during the Salem Witch Trials. In truth, the majority were hanged. *Hangings are cleaner. You don't have to listen to the screams when it turns out they were innocent.*

❯ Noel Botham, *The Mega Book of Useless Information* (John Blake, 2009), 182.

The first e-mail was sent by Ray Tomlinson in 1971 between two computers that were actually right next to each other. *He simply sent it to his best friend: his other computer.*

❯ Mary Bellis, "History of Email & Ray Tomlinson," About.com, *www.inventors.about.com.*

General Ulysses S. Grant detested almost all forms of military music and revelry. He claimed to only recognize two tunes. "One was 'Yankee Doodle.' The other one wasn't." *He was also kind of a turd.*

❯ "Civil War Fact Sheet," PBS, *www.pbs.org.*

Both George Washington and Thomas Jefferson grew marijuana plants on their farms for use as hemp. Jefferson even drafted the Declaration of Independence on hemp paper. *He would have finished it sooner, but he smoked the first two drafts.*

❯ "History Facts," North American Industrial Hemp Council, *www.naihc.org.*

While it's true that George Washington called for the emancipation of his slaves in his will, he stipulated that this would not occur until the death of his wife Martha. When she drafted her own will, she chose not to free them. *Hear that? It's the sound of me not touching this one with a 1,000-foot pole.*

❭ Terry L. Jordan, *The U.S. Constitution and Fascinating Facts About It* (Oak Hill Publishing Co., 1999), 15.

During World War II, the Bicycle Playing Card company sent special playing card decks as gifts to POWs in Germany. Unbeknownst to their captors, when moistened the cards revealed precise escape routes for the prisoners. *I firmly believe humans were at least five times smarter in the 1940s.*

❭ "The History of Bicycle Cards," Bicycle Cards, w*ww.bicycle cards.com.*

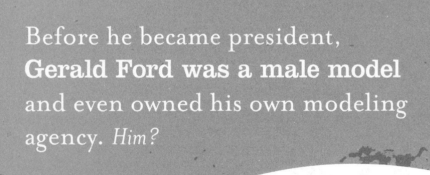

Before he became president, **Gerald Ford was a male model** and even owned his own modeling agency. *Him?*

❭ Ethan Lou, "6 Presidential Secrets Your History Teacher Didn't Mention," *Cracked,* January 4, 2011, *www.cracked.com.*

To fill the near-empty Morena Dam reservoir, the city of San Diego approached notable "rainmaker" Charles Hatfield for his services in 1916. Unprepared for the resulting deluge, the city was plagued by massive flooding, resulting in millions of dollars of damages. *Be careful what you wish for.*

> Alan Bellows, "Rainmakers and Cloudbusters," Damn Interesting, October 25, 2005, *www.damninteresting.com.*

Charles Hatfield was never able to accept payment for his stunning feat of rainmaking. The city of San Diego claimed that, should he accept the money, he would admit he caused the rain and would thus be responsible for any damages. *If you invite a horse over for breakfast, don't complain when it shits in your cereal.*

> Alan Bellows, "Rainmakers and Cloudbusters," Damn Interesting, October 25, 2005, *www.damninteresting.com.*

The first airplane journey across the continental United States took forty-nine days. *I'd argue it doesn't count if you have to land.*

> *Weird but True! 3: 300 Outrageous Facts* (*National Geographic* Children's Books, 2011), 13.

Comedian Russell Brand was fired from MTV when he wore an Osama Bin Laden costume on September 12, 2001. *I'm offended not as an American but as a humorist.*

> Russell Brand, "And Then I Became a Junkie," *The Guardian*, November 12, 2007, *www.guardian.co.uk.*

Georgia's Oglethorpe University is home to one of the most ambitious time capsule projects in human history. Sealed in 1940, "The Crypt of Civilization" contains various human artifacts from a mundane can opener and women's underwear to recordings of historical leaders and famous works of literature. The airtight vault is not scheduled to be opened until the year 8113. *I'm sure our robot overlords will find it very amusing.*

❯ "The Crypt of Civilization at Oglethorpe University," Oglethorpe University, *www.oglethorpe.edu.*

Rough and Ready, California, officially seceded from the Union in 1850 but promptly voted to return when bartenders in surrounding communities refused to serve noncitizens. *If there's a problem that alcohol can't solve, I'd like to hear it.*

❯ Tim O'Brian, "Let Freedom (and Strange July 4th Facts) Ring! Ripley's Believe It or Not! Chronicles Independence Day Oddities, Such as When the Liberty Bell 'Really' Rang For the First Time!," *Ripley's Newsroom*, June 13, 2011, *www.ripleysnewsroom.com.*

Before the 2003 invasion of Iraq, the CIA briefly debated flooding the country with a faked video depicting Saddam Hussein having sex with a teenage boy. *If you're sad it never got made, rest assured something similar exists in the seedy underbelly of the Internet.*

❯ Jeff Stein, "CIA Unit's Wacky Idea: Depict Saddam as Gay," *The Washington Post*, May 25, 2010, *www.washingtonpost .com.*

After Abraham Lincoln was assassinated, Vice President Andrew Johnson stepped up to take the presidential oath of office—completely drunk. *In his defense, the last guy didn't fare so well sober.*

❯ "The Discovernator," Discovery Channel, *www .news.discovery.com.*

Play-Doh was originally sold as a wallpaper cleaner by Kutol Products, a Cincinnati soap company. It was not until they noticed local nursery school children using the product to make Christmas ornaments that they decided to market it as a children's toy. *It also tastes pretty good. Not that I'd know . . .*

❯ Tim Walsh, *Timeless Toys: Classic Toys and the Playmakers Who Created Them* (Andrews McMeel, 2005), 115–117.

In the late nineteenth century, Bayer marketed heroin as a cough medicine. *It didn't work, but nobody cared.*

❯ "The Discovernator," Discovery Channel, *www.news.discovery.com*.

After the attack on Pearl Harbor, the United States distributed specially marked currency bills, called "Hawaii overprint notes," to the islands. The theory was that if Hawaii was invaded by the Japanese, the currency would then become invalid. *Just like real money, but with double the fear.*

❯ John Farrier, "Hawaiian Dollars," Neatorama, October 9, 2011, *www.neatorama.com*.

The ivory gavel currently in use by the United States Senate is actually a replica. The original was used from as early as 1789 until 1954, when Richard Nixon broke it during a heated debate over nuclear energy. *Just throwing this out there, but perhaps they shouldn't have used the 165-year-old priceless antique in their daily activities.*

❯ "The Senate's New Gavel," The United States Senate, *www.senate.gov*.

Due to his declining physical health, during the Constitutional Convention of 1787, Ben Franklin entered the convention hall for meetings in a sedan chair carried by four prisoners from the Walnut Street Jail in Philadelphia. *May he who would not enjoy being carried to work cast the first stone.*

> ❯ Terry L. Jordan, *The U.S. Constitution and Fascinating Facts About It* (Oak Hill Publishing Co., 1999), 28.

America's love affair with alcohol is not a new phenomenon by any stretch of the imagination. By 1830, the average American over the age of fifteen drank the equivalent of eighty-eight bottles of whiskey a year. *Might explain why a fifty-year-old man was considered ancient at the time.*

> ❯ Tan Vinh, "PBS 'Prohibition' Features Seattle Bootlegger," *The Seattle Times*, October 1, 2011," www.seattletimes.com.

George Washington initially wished to be called "His Mightiness, the President." The title was abandoned in favor of "Mr. President." *More modest, sure, but infinitely less badass.*

> ❯ Erin Barrett and Jack Mingo, *Random Kinds Of Factness: 1001 (or So) Absolutely True Tidbits About (Mostly) Everything* (Conari Press, 2005), 4.

The USA PATRIOT Act is an acronym. It stands for Uniting and Strengthening America by Providing Appropriate Tools Required to Intercept and Obstruct Terrorism. *Of course it does.*

> ❯ "Public Law 107 - 56 - Uniting and Strengthening America by Providing Appropriate Tools Required to Intercept and Obstruct Terrorism (USA PATRIOT Act) Act of 2001," U.S. Government Printing Office, www.gpo.gov.

On August 5, 2006, NASA revealed that it had lost—or possibly taped over—several videos of the original *Apollo 11* moon landing. Despite an extensive search, the tapes have not yet been recovered. *Perhaps the agency doesn't deserve funding after all.*

> Leonard David, "Apollo TV Tapes: the Search Continues," Space.com, November 3, 2006, *www.space.com.*

After his death, the remains of British revolutionary Thomas Paine were purchased by a journalist named William Cobbett, who tried to raise money to give him a proper burial in England. When he couldn't raise the funds, Cobbett kept the body in a trunk in his attic. *Please, for the love of whatever deity you do or do not believe in, go draft a will.*

> Christopher Shay, "Top 10 Famous Stolen Body Parts," *Time*, May 12, 2010, *www.time.com.*

The first ever transorbital lobotomy was performed by psychiatrist Walter Freeman in his Washington, D.C., office on January 17, 1946. Before his death in 1972, he performed the procedure on approximately 2,500 patients. *If you can think of a better way to cure intelligence, I'd like to hear it.*

> "'My Lobotomy': Howard Dully's Journey," NPR, November 16, 2005, *www.npr.org.*

One of Walter Freeman's youngest patients was a twelve-year-old boy named Howard Dully. His stepmother's main complaints were that he was "defiant" and "objects to going to bed." *So her child was acting like a child?*

> "'My Lobotomy': Howard Dully's Journey," NPR, November 16, 2005, *www.npr.org.*

The first Thanksgiving lasted three days and consisted of ninety Wampanoag Indians and about fifty Pilgrims. There were no women present, and it is unlikely that anybody ate turkey. *Poor bastards probably didn't even know what Stovetop was.*

❯ Robert Krulwich, "First Thanksgiving Dinner: No Turkeys. No Ladies. No Pies.," NPR, November 22, 2010, *www.npr.org.*

Social convention in the late 1800s dictated that boys wear dresses until around the age of six or seven. Pink was also deemed a more socially acceptable color for boys than girls until the 1940s. *Popped collars have always been gender neutrally obnoxious.*

❯Jeanne Maglaty, "When Did Girls Start Wearing Pink," *Smithsonian* magazine, April 8, 2011, *www.smithsonianmag.com.*

Somewhere at the bottom of the ocean off the coast of Georgia rests a 7,000-pound nuclear bomb. A B-47 bomber inadvertently dropped it in 1958 after it collided with another air force jet. *Shh, don't tell North Korea.*

❯ "For 50 years, Nuclear Bomb Lost in Watery Grave," NPR, February 3, 2008, *www.npr.org.*

The first novel ever written on a typewriter was *The Adventures of Tom Sawyer* by Mark Twain. *Side note: Typing on a modern-day typewriter does not make you sophisticated. It makes you a douche.*

❯ "The Discovernator," Discovery Channel, *www.news .discovery.com.*

When CBS broadcast its first television show in color, there were no privately owned color television sets. *Small oversight.*

> Noel Botham, *The Bumper Book of Useless Information* (John Blake, 2008), 167.

During Einstein's autopsy, the pathologist at Princeton Hospital removed his brain in the hopes that future neuroscientists would be able to unlock the secret of his intelligence. *Not like he was using it at the time.*

> "The Long, Strange Journey of Einstein's Brain," NPR, April 18, 2005, *www.npr.org.*

Einstein's eyes currently sit in a safe deposit box in New York City. *Thankfully the rest of his body was cremated. Otherwise it would be off spinning somewhere.*

> "The Long, Strange Journey of Einstein's Brain," NPR, April 18, 2005, *www.npr.org.*

In 2001, American millionaire Denis Tito became the first space tourist. He paid $20 million to spend a week on the International Space Station. *Sure he could have used the money to feed the nation's homeless, but floating around in space was way cooler.*

> Russell Ash, *Firefly's World of Facts* (Firefly Books, 2007), 220.

During his career, **Thomas Edison** held an astounding 1,093 patents. *Sure, but back then you could poop into aluminum foil and call it a machine.*

> "The Discovernator," Discovery Channel, *www.news.discovery.com.*

During their travels across the country, explorers Lewis and Clark often traded with Native American tribes for food, which frequently included dog meat. By the end of their journey, they had developed quite the taste for man's best friend, to the point that Lewis claimed to prefer it over venison or elk. *Tastes like chicken, only cuter.*

> Bill Lawrence, *Fascinating Facts from American History* (J. Weston Walch, 1985), 44.

Until the September 11 attacks on the Twin Towers, the worst terror incident in New York City history was the 1920 bombing that occurred at the corner of Wall Street and Broad Street. A lone individual loaded a wagon with explosives and pulled it to "The Corner" by horse before igniting the payload and escaping on foot. The resulting blast killed thirty-nine people and injured hundreds more. *That poor horse.*

> Daniel Gross, "Previous Terror on Wall Street—a Look at a 1920 Bombing," *The Street,* September 20, 2001, *www.thestreet.com.*

The last pirate hanged in America was Albert E. Hicks, who was executed before a crowd of 10,000 on July 13, 1860. *That's what this country's been missing. I couldn't put my finger on it.*

❯ Ian Harrison, *Take Me to Your Leader* (Dorling Kindersley Ltd., 2007), 333.

The first copyrighted film in U.S. history was of Thomas Edison's assistant sneezing. *The deleted scene where he lights a fart on fire is breathtaking.*

❯ "Edison Kinetoscopic Record of a Sneeze, January 7, 1894/ W.K.L. Dickson," Library of Congress, *www.loc.gov.*

When the Pilgrims arrived in Plymouth, several of the Native Americans they encountered already spoke English. *The modern day equivalent of meeting aliens who listen to Ke$ha.*

❯ "Native American Perspective: Fast Turtle, Wampanoag Tribe Member," Scholastic, *www.scholastic.com.*

In 1989, an unnamed bargain hunter purchased a $4 painting from a flea market only to discover an old piece of parchment wedged between the canvas and the frame. As it turned out, the brittle document was actually an original copy of the Declaration of Independence worth more than $8 million. *The original owner of the painting later died from a severe case of hindsight.*

❯ Steve Berges, *Founding Fathers Fun Facts: And Other U.S. Trivia* (American Liberty Press, 2010), 26.

President Martin Van Buren's autobiography does not once mention his wife. *The power of denial is an extraordinary thing.*

❯ Neal Finkelstein, PhD, *U.S. Presidents Fun Facts and Word Search* (lulu.com, 2008), 18.

Preindustrial Americans often experienced two distinct patterns of sleep during the night. After retiring for "first sleep" at around 9:00 P.M., early Americans woke up around midnight to smoke a pipe or converse with neighbors for several hours before retiring for "second sleep." *Today I learned the colonists were hobbits.*

❯ A. Roger Ekirch, "Dreams Deferred," *The New York Times*, February 19, 2006, *www.nytimes.com*.

Born in 1924, **Jimmy Carter** was the first president to come into the world via a hospital. *The rest were cloned in labs.*

❯ "Oct 1, 1924: Jimmy Carter is Born," History Channel, *www.history.com*.

The iconic Christmas song "Jingle Bells" was originally intended to be an ode to Thanksgiving. *This fact does not make the song any less irritating, though.*

❯ Stacy Conradt, "'Jingle Bells' was Originally Written for Thanksgiving," Mental Floss, November 23, 2011, *www.mentalfloss.com*.

By the end of the Civil War, as much as one half of all paper currency in circulation was counterfeit. *Today it's all real, but still worthless.*

❯ Noel Botham, *The Mega Book of Useless Information* (John Blake, 2009), 332.

After a crime spree that spanned three years, the reign of terror Bonnie Parker and Clyde Barrow spread over the Midwest came to an abrupt halt on May 23, 1934. As the couple drove through Bienville Parish, they were ambushed by a team of six officers who fired 167 rounds into the car, killing the couple. *The first twenty were warranted. The last 147 were just for fun.*

❯ Paul Rosa, "The Story of Bonnie and Clyde," History Buff, *www.historybuff.com.*

As many as fifty rounds smashed into the bodies of Bonnie Parker and Clyde Barrow on the day of their deaths. When officers ceased fire to inspect the car, they found that the fingers on Bonnie's right hand had been shot clean away. *Probably best she didn't survive that one.*

❯ Paul Rosa, "The Story of Bonnie and Clyde," History Buff, *www.historybuff.com.*

At the time they were killed by police in 1934, Bonnie and Clyde were believed to be responsible for thirteen murders, nine of which were of police officers. *And the other four kind of looked like police officers.*

❯ "Bonnie and Clyde," Federal Bureau of Investigation, *www.fbi.gov.*

In 1916, the House of Representatives shot down a bill that would have put all acts of war to a national vote, with anyone voting yes being required to register for service in the U.S. military. *Too bad. We could use more game theory in our voting process.*

❯ "Proposed Amendments," Constitution Facts, *www.constitutionfacts.com*.

In July 1744, British colonists paid $2,400 to the Iroquois Indians for the land that is now upstate New York. As it turned out, the Iroquois had no claim on the land. The colonists had been tricked and soon found themselves warring with other Native American tribes over the land they thought they had purchased. *Touché, Iroquois. Touché.*

❯ George W. Givens, *500 Little-Known Facts in U.S. History* (Cedar Fort, 2006), 73.

In the 1920s, Philadelphia Mayor J. Hampton Moore assembled a "smelling squad" to patrol the banks of the Schuylkill and Delaware rivers and determine the cause of the city's offensive odor. *Unfortunately, they did not possess enough deodorizer to cleanse the entire state of New Jersey.*

❯ "A Member of the Philadelphia 'Smelling Squad' on Frankford Creek, Philadelphia, PA, Circa 1930," Explore PA History, *www.explorepahistory.com*.

Justice Byron "Whizzer" White was the first and only Supreme Court justice to be inducted into the Football Hall of Fame. *We all know which is the greater honor . . .*

❯ Terry L. Jordan, *The U.S. Constitution and Fascinating Facts About It* (Oak Hill Publishing Co., 1999), 78.

When returning from the moon,
astronauts Buzz Aldrin, Michael Collins, and Neil Armstrong had to pass through customs. *How does one declare "swagger"?*

❯ "The Discovernator," Discovery Channel, *www.news .discovery.com.*

Along with a plaque and an American flag,
the astronauts of *Apollo 11* left behind some 5,000 pounds of cameras, tools, and debris when they left the moon in 1969. *If we didn't leave behind garbage, nobody would believe humans had ever been there.*

❯ Bill Lawrence, *Fascinating Facts from American History* (J. Weston Walch, 1985), 231.

The *Apollo* astronauts were quarantined for twenty-one days upon their return to Earth, for fear they might have been infected with an alien virus. *Better safe than zombies.*

❯ "The Discovernator," Discovery Channel, *www.news.discovery.com.*

Neil Armstrong may have been the first man to set foot on the surface of the moon, but the honor of the first lunar urination belongs to his partner Buzz Aldrin. Using his suit's built-in collection device, Aldrin emptied his bladder shortly after stepping out of the lunar module. *When you gotta go, you gotta go.*

> Bill Lawrence, *Fascinating Facts from American History* (J. Weston Walch, 1985), 230.

Six percent of Americans do not believe we actually landed on the moon. *Yet 92 percent believe a bearded man in the sky listens to their problems. Go figure.*

> Christina Caron, "Refuting the Most Popular Apollo Moon Landing Hoax Theories," ABC News, July 19, 2009, *www.abcnews.go.com.*

Alan Shepard was the first and only person to play golf on the moon. *Why explore when you can dick around?*

> Noel Botham, *The Bumper Book of Useless Information* (John Blake, 2008), 341.

After the defeat of the Nazis in World War II, the Soviet Union presented a wooden replica of the Great Seal of the United States to Ambassador Averell Harriman, who hung it in his office. Eight years later, a routine inspection revealed the gift contained a bugging device the Soviets had used to spy on the ambassador. *Well played, you lovable commie bastards. Well played.*

> "The Great Seal Bug Story," Spy Busters, *www.spybusters.com.*

In 1851, physician Samuel A. Cartwright proposed that African slaves who felt a compulsion to flee from their masters suffered from a mental illness he called drapetomania. His theory was widely believed and republished in numerous medical journals of the day. *Well, that's enough research for one day.*

> "Top 10 Shocking Historical Beliefs and Practices," Listverse, November 23, 2010, *www.listverse.com.*

During an especially rough winter in 1609 early European colonists in present-day Virginia were forced to resort to cannibalism. *Which is why you should never be the fattest friend.*

> Jill Harness, "Little Known Facts about American History," Neatorama, February 25, 2010, *www.neatorama.com.*

In 1938, *Time* magazine named **Adolf Hitler** as their Man of the Year. *Whoops.*

> "Adolf Hitler: Man of the Year, 1938," *Time*, January 2, 1939, *www.time.com.*

When the infamous Donner party left Springfield, Illinois, to emigrate to California in 1846, the group consisted of eighty-nine settlers. After numerous missteps, the party found themselves trapped high in the Sierra Nevada Mountains and were forced to resort to cannibalism to survive. Only forty-five members made it out alive. *Would have been forty-six*
if some people hadn't insisted on seconds.

> "Donner Party," History Channel, *www.history.com.*

The 342 chests of tea tossed into Boston Harbor during the Boston Tea Party were valued at $36,000, which would translate to more than $400,000 today. *You can be an American or you can be a person who drinks tea. You can't be both.*

> Jan Payne, *The World's Best Book: The Spookiest, Smelliest, Wildest, Oldest, Weirdest, Brainiest, and Funniest Facts* (Running Press Kids, 2009).

In the late 1800s, only 15 percent of all residents of American cities had access to indoor bathrooms. *You may live in a roach-infested, dingy closet of an apartment, but at least you can poop inside.*

> Erin Barrett and Jack Mingo, *Random Kinds Of Factness: 1001 (or So) Absolutely True Tidbits About (Mostly) Everything* (Conari Press, 2005), 4.

On July 20, 2002, NASA intern Thad Roberts stole 101 grams of priceless moon rocks from the Johnson Space Center in Houston, Texas. He then retreated to an Orlando hotel where he allegedly scattered the rocks on the bed and had sex with his girlfriend on top of them. *In all seriousness, what else should he have done with them?*

> "How One Man Had Sex on the Moon," Canadian Broadcasting Corporation, August 4, 2011, *www.cbc.ca.*

Thad Roberts would later be arrested while trying to sell his ill-gotten moon rocks to a Belgian mineralist. He served seven and a half years in federal prison for his crime. *Not sure where "perverted rock thief" falls in the prison pecking order.*

> "How One Man Had Sex on the Moon," Canadian Broadcasting Corporation, August 4, 2011, *www.cbc.ca.*

CHAPTER 12

Only in America
The Strangest Happenings of the Strangest Country of All

As hard as you might try, it's impossible to classify every weird happening in the history of the United States. But this does not mean these miscellaneous oddities are not worth mentioning. If anything, they are the most interesting facts I managed to uncover.

So without pretense and with minimal preamble, I give you the strangest of the strange. The most bizarre of the bizarre. The crème de la crème of useless weird American trivia. Please enjoy in moderation.

The United States Department of Defense is the largest employer in the world.

To be fair, a lot of people really hate us.

❯ "Who Are the World's Biggest Employers?" *The Economist*, September 12, 2011, *www.economist.com.*

Sold in the 1950s and 1960s, the Atomic Energy Lab kit produced by the American Basic Science Club wasn't just a toy—it was actually radioactive. The kit came with real samples of uranium and radium for children to experiment with. *"Look Mommy, my face is peeling just like the kid on the box!"*

❯ "The 8 Most Wildly Irresponsible Vintage Toys," *Cracked*, October 19, 2001, *www.cracked .com.*

Apple Store employees are forbidden from correcting customers who mispronounce the names of the company's products. *"One MacPadPhonePod please."*

❯ Brett Ryder, "The Art of Selling," *The Economist*, October 22, 2011, *www.economist.com.*

The Zolp Scholarship is available only to college-bound students planning to attend Chicago's Loyola University who happen to be named Zolp. *A small consolation for a lifetime of emotional scarring.*

❯ David Wallechinsky, *The Book Of Lists: The Original Compendium of Curious Information* (Canongate Books, 2009).

A 2009 study conducted by the American Mustache Institute found that mustached men earned 8.2 percent more than their bearded counterparts, and 4.3 percent more than clean-shaven men. *According to the Society for People Named Eric Grzymkowski, I am 200 percent better looking than everyone else. Combined.*

❯ Edward J. Carr, "Study: Men with Mustaches Make More Money," NBC New York, October 10, 2009, *www.nbcnewyork .com*.

During World War II, the United States government tried to sneak estrogen into Hitler's food to make his mustache fall off and change his masculine voice into a comical soprano. They hoped he would then be laughed out of power. The plan was a failure, as the gardener they bribed to carry out the deed never followed through. *All things considered, it really is amazing that we won that war.*

❯ David Wallechinsky, *The Book Of Lists: The Original Compendium of Curious Information* (Canongate Books, 2009).

There is no such thing as a "Congressional Medal of Honor." There is simply a Medal of Honor that happens to be awarded by Congress. *Also, there's no such thing as fairies, Santa is your mom and dad, and only some dogs go to heaven. Sorry, kids.*

❯ Jamie Frater, *Listverse.com's Ultimate Book of Bizarre Lists: Fascinating Facts and Shocking Trivia on Movies, Music, Crime, Celebrities, History, and More* (Ulysses Press, 2010), 181–182.

If it appears the actors in Ridley Scott's *Alien* were genuinely surprised to see a creature burst forth from John Hurt's chest, it's because they were. Scott purposely kept them in the dark to capture a more genuine reaction. *And because it was way funnier for him that way.*

❯ Bo Moore, "10 Fantastic Movie Scenes That Were More Real Than You Knew," *Paste* magazine, April 8, 2011, *www .pastemagazine.com*.

Americans take a collective 18 billion elevator trips each year. Despite that fact, only about twenty-seven people die annually in elevator accidents. *And most of them are pretty old anyway.*

> Tina Susman, "Elevator Accident Kills Woman In Manhattan; Such Events Are Rare, *Los Angeles Times*, December 14, 2011, *www.latimes.com*.

Eighty-nine percent of **pornography** distributed throughout the world is produced in the United States. *And people complain we don't export anything useful.*

> Michael Arrington, "Internet Pornography Stats," Tech Crunch, May 12, 2007, *www.techcrunch.com*.

In 2006, 16 million Americans underwent some form of cosmetic surgery. *And the world is a more attractive place thanks to their noble sacrifice.*

> Jessica Williams, *50 Facts That Should Change the World 2.0* (The Disinformation Company, 2007), 61.

Cleveland's Cuyahoga River is arguably the nation's most polluted waterway. The river is more than 50 percent acid and industrial waste in some areas and has caught fire on multiple occasions. *Another reason to never get within 100 miles of Cleveland.*

> Bruce Felton and Mark Fowler, *The Best, Worst, & Most Unusual: Noteworthy Achievements, Events, Feats & Blunders of Every Conceivable Kind* (Galahad, 2004), 265.

Cap'n Crunch's **real name** is Captain Horatio Magellan Crunch.

Because the fictional character on my cereal box needs a back story.

> Jason English, "Real Names of 23 Fictional Characters," CNN, June 13, 2010, *www.cnn.com*.

About 11 percent of Americans between the ages of eighteen and twenty-four cannot locate the United States on a map of the world. More than two-thirds can't pinpoint the United Kingdom, and only a paltry 15 percent can locate Iraq. *Before you judge, ask yourself this: Do I know where Vietnam is?*

> Bijal P. Trivedi, "Survey Reveals Geographic Illiteracy," *National Geographic*, November 20, 2002, *www.news.nationalgeographic.com*.

On average, every week in the United States five parents are killed by their biological children. *Better they do it quick and painlessly than slowly over the course of a lifetime.*

> "Q&A: Why Kids Kill Parents," CBS News, *www.cbsnews.com*.

The **average bra size** for an American woman is 36C. *But remember, ladies, no matter what size you are, we will always be fascinated by them.*

> Ana Marie Cox, "If Your Bra Doesn't Fit, Go Shopping," *Time*, June 27, 2006, *www.time.com*.

The native **Hawaiian alphabet** has only thirteen letters. *But they generally only use four: S, P, A, and M.*

❯ *Weird but True! 3: 300 Outrageous Facts* (National Geographic Children's Books, 2011), 62.

Alaska is both the westernmost and easternmost state. Some of Alaska's Aleutian Islands are actually in the eastern hemisphere, west of the 180th meridian. *Call me when it has a record for something besides existing.*

❯ Joey Green, *Contrary to Popular Belief: More Than 250 False Facts Revealed* (Broadway Books, 2005), 13.

The average American produces about **4.3 pounds of waste** per day. *But you should always strive to be above average.*

❯ "Municipal Solid Waste," United States Environmental Protection Agency, *www.epa.gov.*

Until the summer of 2000, a lone pay telephone could be found smack in the middle of California's Mojave Desert at the intersection of two small dirt roads. The phone booth became a pilgrimage site for thousands of curious travelers who journeyed to the remote location to answer calls coming in from all around the world. *Creepy side fact: There are people reading this who have never seen a pay phone in the wild.*

> "The Mojave Phone Booth," BBC, August 16th, 2006, *www.bbc.co.uk.*

Autoerotic asphyxiation

kills more than 500 Americans each year.

Darwinism in action.

> "Ten Weird Human Sex Facts," Divine Caroline, *www.divine caroline.com.*

The average lifespan of a major league baseball is only seven pitches. *Don't worry, afterwards they go to live on a farm with your childhood pets.*

> "The Discovernator," Discovery Channel, *www.news .discovery.com.*

Although some of New York City's crosswalk buttons are still active, the vast majority were rendered useless in the 1980s. Of the 3,250 still in use, more than 2,500 serve as nothing more than mechanical placebos. *Don't worry, the "close door" button on the elevator totally works.*

> Michael Luo, "For Exercise in New York Futility, Push Button," *The New York Times*, February 27, 2004, *www.nytimes.com.*

To intimidate their opponents, members of the 1982 men's University of Pittsburgh Rugby Club brought some unconventional equipment to practice with them before a match against Juniata College— severed human heads. As a result, the team was banished from campus sports for eight years. *Eight years is not enough. Eight hundred years is not enough.*

❯ "Unbelievable Rugby Trivia," University of Western Sydney, *www.uwshawkesbury.rugby .net.au*

Organized crime accounts for about 10 percent of total income in the United States. *Humor book writing accounts for .00000000000001 percent.*

❯ Noel Botham, *The Bumper Book of Useless Information* (John Blake, 2008), 202.

❯ Pustak Mahal, *501 Astonishing Facts* (Pustak Mahal, 2010).

The world's largest recorded hailstone fell in Coffeyville, Kansas, on September 3, 1970. It weighed 1.67 pounds and measured seven and a half inches in diameter. *I could possibly care less, but I'd have to try really hard.*

Before the fiftieth printing of his electrocardiography textbook, Dr. Dale Dubin hid the following message for students to find: "Congratulations for your perseverance. You may win the car on page 46 by writing down your name and address and submitting it to the publisher." Of the 60,000 copies purchased, only five students submitted their names to claim the prize. *If only he had hidden the message in the CliffsNotes version of his book.*

❯ "Salted Treat," Snopes, *www.snopes.com.*

About one-third of all **homicides committed** in the United States go unsolved. *I like those odds.*

❯ Thomas Hangrove, "Unsolved Murder Rate Increasing," News Channel Five, May 3, 2010, *www.newsnet5.com*.

In Greece, actor Charlton Heston is credited as "Charlton Easton," due to the scatological image evoked by the word *heston* in Greek. *I won't tell you exactly what it means. That's what Google is for.*

❯ "Charlton Heston," IMDb, *www.imdb.com*.

In 1980, employees at a Las Vegas hospital were suspended when it came to light that the group had been betting on when patients would die. *I don't see a problem—unless of course they rigged the results . . .*

❯ "The Discovernator," Discovery Channel, *www.news .discovery.com*.

The average American teenager

sends and receives 3,339 text messages each month. *If only we could harness that wasted energy.*

❯ "Average American Teen Sends and Receives 3,339 Texts A Month," MSNBC, October 14, 2010, *www.msnbc.msn.com*.

In 2005, the **National Toy Hall of Fame** inducted the cardboard box into its illustrious list. *If the cardboard box is a toy, so is my toothbrush.*

> "Cardboard Box," National Toy Hall of Fame, *www.toyhalloffame.org.*

The Library of Congress has produced a Braille version of every *Playboy* magazine since 1970. *If there is a heaven, there will be a special place reserved for these brave individuals.*

> "The Magazine Program of the National Library Service for the Blind and Physically Handicapped (NLS)," Library of Congress, 2007, *www.loc.gov.*

As of 2005, **one in five Americans** believed the sun revolves around the earth. *If this fact surprises you, then you are the idiot.*

> Cornelia Dean, "Scientific Savvy? In U.S., Not Much," *The New York Times,* August 30, 2005, *www.nytimes.com.*

Alaska has the highest suicide rate, at twenty-two individuals per 100,000 annually. *If you have ever spent time in Alaska, this should not surprise you.*

❯ Bourree Lam, "Suicide vs. Homicide by State, per 100,000," Freakonomics, September 1, 2011, *www.freakonomics.com*.

Americans who refuse to accept the inevitability of death can have their bodies frozen at the Cryonics Institute in Clinton Township, Michigan. Although the technology to unfreeze a customer does not currently exist, the company is optimistic it will become available in the future. *Minor detail.*

❯ Stephanie Pappas, "8 Alternative Burial Technologies That Are Going Mainstream," Fox News, September 13, 2011, *www.foxnews.com*.

Thrifty patrons of the Cryonics Institute can avoid the hefty $200,000 price tag for a full body freezing and opt instead to have only their heads frozen. The cost for that procedure is a paltry $80,000. *How much for a head minus the frontal lobe? I don't use it much anyway.*

❯ Stephanie Pappas, "8 Alternative Burial Technologies That Are Going Mainstream," Fox News, September 13, 2011, *www.foxnews.com*.

As of 2011, there were more than 200 individuals in cryogenic storage in the United States. *They are either the smartest or dumbest 200 Americans in history.*

❯ Stephanie Pappas, "8 Alternative Burial Technologies That Are Going Mainstream," Fox News, September 13, 2011, *www.foxnews.com*.

On average, American men have a penis that is 6.5 inches long when aroused. *If your boyfriend insists he's never measured, dump him immediately. He's a liar.*

> Dr. David Delvin and Christine Webber, "Facts About Penis Size," Net Doctor, *www.netdoctor.co.uk.*

In 1970, the U.S. Consumer Product Safety Commission printed 80,000 promotional buttons with the slogan, "Think Toy Safety." To their horror, they soon discovered the button's metal tab fasteners broke off to create sharp edges and could easily be swallowed by children. They were also coated with lead paint. *In their defense, a button is hardly a toy.*

> David Wallechinsky, *The Book Of Lists: The Original Compendium of Curious Information* (Canongate Books, 2009).

Americans **Google** the word "poop" more than any other country does.

It's actually just one guy over and over again.

> "Poop," Google Trends, *www.google.com/trends.*

The three most popular passwords Americans use to safeguard their e-mails are "123456," "qwerty," and "abc123." *It's not "hacking" if your target happens to be an idiot.*

> Ashlee Vance, "If Your Password Is 123456, Just Make It Hackme," *The New York Times*, January 20, 2010, *www.nytimes.com.*

Richard Milhous Nixon was the first U.S. president whose name contained all of the letters in the word "criminal." *It's our own fault for electing him despite such concrete evidence of his questionable character.*

> David Darling, *The Universal Book of Mathematics: From Abracadabra to Zeno's Paradoxes* (Wiley, 2004), 351.

Due to its general inability to stick to a surface, the weak glue found in Post-it notes was deemed a failure when it was first invented by Spencer Silver in 1969. It wasn't until five years later when a colleague used it to prevent page markers from falling out of his hymnal that Spencer realized its potential. *It's still kind of a failure.*

> Ian Harrison, *Take Me to Your Leader* (Dorling Kindersley Ltd., 2007), 315.

The world's tallest mountain is not Mt. Everest, but instead Mauna Loa in Hawaii, which rises 33,476 feet from the sea floor. However only about 14,000 feet is visible above sea level. *It's way easier to climb, too.*

> Pustak Mahal, *501 Astonishing Facts* (Pustak Mahal, 2010).

There are three power grids in the continental United States: the Eastern Interconnection powers the easternmost states, the Western Interconnection powers the westernmost states, and ERCOT powers Texas. *Just in case somebody messes with them.*

> Kate Galbraith, "Texplainer: Why Does Texas Have Its Own Power Grid?," *The Texas Tribune*, February 8, 2011, *www.texas tribune.org.*

The full name of Los Angeles is
El Pueblo de Nuestra Señora la Reina de los Angeles de Porciúncula. In English it means "The Town of Our Lady the Queen of the Angels of the River Porciúncula." *Just rolls right off the tongue.*

❯ Trivia, The Real Name of Los Angeles," Neatorama, January 6, 2008, *www.neatorama.com*.

Until 1924, Native American individuals living in the United States were not considered official citizens of the country. It was not until Congress passed the Indian Citizenship Act of 1924 that Native Americans were given full rights as citizens. *Kind of a hollow victory. A bit like having the umpire declare you safe three hundred years after your last Little League game.*

❯ "1924 Indian Citizenship Act," Nebraskastudies.org, *www .nebraskastudies.org*.

Original copies of the first Super Special KISS comic

books printed in 1977 contain trace amounts of blood from members of the band. *Least. Surprising. Fact. Ever.*

❯ "Blood Money," Snopes, *www.snopes.com*.

To prove the blood in their comic actually belonged to the members of KISS, the band hired a notary to verify that phials they added to the vat of red dye in the printing plant were actually their own. *When I think integrity, I think KISS.*

❯ "Blood Money," Snopes, *www.snopes.com*.

Until 2009, Disneyland employed an individual whose sole responsibility was to review pictures taken on the popular Splash Mountain ride and remove those that contained exposed breasts or genitalia. Park officials reassigned the position when they realized few park goers actually flashed the camera. *My dreams of becoming a professional boob inspector have turned to ash.*

> Danny Gallagher and JD Niemand, "6 True Stories about Disneyland They Don't Want You to Know," *Cracked*, April 29, 2010, *www.cracked.com.*

The average American uses fifty pounds of toilet paper a year. *My philosophy: It's not clean until there's blood.*

> Linda Rodriguez , "Why Toilet Paper Belongs to America," CNN, July 7, 2009, *www.cnn.com.*

Only one child since 1974 has died as a result of poisoned Halloween candy. His father did it. *Not the best way to get all your kid's candy for yourself, but effective.*

> "The Discovernator," Discovery Channel, *www.news.discovery.com.*

The Anderson-McQueen funeral home in St. Petersburg, Florida, is the only place in the United States where customers can choose to have their remains dissolved; through a process called resomation, a combination of heated water and potassium hydroxide liquefies soft tissue. *Or, with the help of your friendly neighborhood serial killer, you can do it yourself with a bathtub full of lye.*

> Stephanie Pappas, "8 Alternative Burial Technologies That Are Going Mainstream," Fox News, September 13, 2011, *www.foxnews.com.*

For just under $2,000, the American company Lifegem will transform the cremated remains of a loved one into a diamond. In 2007, the company created a $200,000 precious stone using hair taken from Ludwig van Beethoven. *Personally, I'd rather be turned into something useful, like McDonald's honey mustard dipping sauce.*

❯ Neela Banerjee, "Precious Life," *Asian Week*, November 22, 2002, www.asianweek.com.

Approximately 20 percent of Americans claim to not enjoy sex.
Sour grapes, methinks.

❯ Noel Botham, *The Mega Book of Useless Information* (John Blake, 2009), 345.

Shortly after the U.S. Parcel Post Service began operation in 1913, four-year-old May Pierstorff became the first child to travel by mail carrier. Her parents attached $.53 worth of stamps to her person and mailed her from Grangeville, Idaho, to her grandparents in Lewiston, Idaho. *Pro Tip: If you can fit them in an approved brown box first, you're good to go.*

❯ Jennifer Rosenberg, "Sending Children by Parcel Post," About .com, June 26, 2008. www .about.com.

Released in 1934, the $100,000 bill remains the largest denomination of American currency ever printed. It bears the image of Woodrow Wilson and is only used for official transactions between Federal Reserve Banks. *I'm no economist, but I think we should just print up a few million of these and solve the debt crisis. Did I mention I'm not an economist?*

❯ "$100,000 Bill, Rare Coins Highlight Boston's World's Fair of Money," *The Huffington Post*, August 12, 2010, www.huffingtonpost.com.

A single $100,000 bill has an estimated value of $1.6 million today. However, it was never circulated to the general public and cannot be legally held by currency note collectors. *That means the $1 bajillion bill my brother sold me in 1989 must be priceless. It has a picture of a narwhal riding a rainbow while eating a slab of bacon, in case you're wondering.*

> "$100,000 Bill, Rare Coins Highlight Boston's World's Fair of Money," *The Huffington Post*, August 12, 2010, *www.huffingtonpost.com*.

At first glance, Mary Veronica's finishing school in Chelsea, New York, is nothing out of the ordinary: Students learn to walk in heels, properly apply makeup, and participate in dance lessons. The catch? Mary's students are all men! Miss Vera's School for Boys Who Want to Dress Like Girls opened its doors in 1996. *Say what you will, it takes a lot of balls to walk around in six-inch stilettos.*

> Clem Richardson, "Mary Veronica's Miss Vera's School for Boys Who Want to Be Girls Is in Session," *New York Daily News*, November 16, 2008, *www.nydailynews.com*.

The **IRS only investigates** about 2 percent of the millions of Americans who fail to file their taxes every year. *So, so, tempting.*

> Christopher Beam, "Taxes, Schmaxes," *Slate*, April 14, 2009, *www.slate.com*.

In 2003, a group of U.S. scientists worried survivors of a worldwide catastrophe might lose humanity's most valuable resource—information. So they worked to encode bacteria to contain the words to the song "It's a Small World After All." *That's a relief. For a moment there, I was worried they'd code something stupid.*

> Natasha McDowell, "Data Stored in Multiplying Bacteria," *New Scientist*, January 2003, www.newscientist.com.

The most lopsided game in college football history took place between Georgia Tech and Cumberland College in 1916. Cumberland had discontinued their football program before the start of the season but failed to inform Georgia Tech. Facing a $3,000 forfeit fee, the school pulled together a ragtag team of thirteen students who lost with an embarrassing final score of 220 to 0. *That's why beer pong is the best sport. The losers get to drink, and the winners play again.*

> Frank Litsky, "In 1916, a Blowout for the Ages," *The New York Times*, October 7, 2006, www.nytimes.com.

During a 1985 ad campaign for Tampax tampons, actress Courteney Cox became the first person on American television to utter the word "period" in reference to menstruation. *The alternate phrase "shark week" has yet to catch on.*

> Courteney Cox, IMDb, www.imdb.com.

In honor of deceased actor Robert Goulet, each year the American Mustache Institute awards the Robert Goulet Memorial Mustached American of the Year award. *The ability to rock a mustache without looking silly should be reward enough.*

> Sarah Anne Hughes, "Herman Cain, Mark Kelly Up for Mustached American of the Year Award," *The Washington Post*, October 10, 2011, www.washingtonpost.com.

Until 2001, Disneyland employees were not permitted to wear their own underwear while dressing in character. Instead, the park provided them with jock straps, cycling shorts, or tights that wouldn't bunch up. *The jock strap is free, but the pubic lice will cost you.*

❯ Danny Gallagher and JD Niemand, "6 True Stories about Disneyland They Don't Want You to Know," *Cracked*, April 29, 2010, *www.cracked.com.*

According to a 2011 survey conducted by the Centers for Disease Control, 1.1 million Americans between the ages of twenty-five and forty-five were still virgins. *The number is actually much higher; it's just easier to lie than admit your failures to a stranger with a clipboard.*

❯ "New CDC Sex Report: Virginity Is Back, Females Try Same Sex More," *Medical News Today*, March 3, 2011, *www.medicalnewstoday.com.*

Twenty-eight percent of American teens have tried some form of illegal drug. *The other 72 percent are lying.*

❯ Jessica Williams, *50 Facts That Should Change the World 2.0* (The Disinformation Company, 2007), 90.

In 2009, a computer glitch caused as many as 13,000 Visa customers to receive an erroneous charge of $23,148,855,308,184,500 on their prepaid Visa debit cards. To add insult to injury, the customers were also assessed a $15 overdraft fee. *The overdraft fee is the least surprising thing I've discovered so far.*

❯ Jason Kessler, "Glitch Hits Visa Users With More Than $23 Quadrillion Charge," CNN, July 15, 2009, *www.cnn.com.*

NFL cheerleaders generally only make between $50 and $75 per game. *They earn most of their money on "side projects." What do you suppose those are?*

❯ "NFL's Cheerleaders Salary," The Richest People, January 3, 2011, *www.therichest.org.*

University of Oregon student Carolyn Davidson designed the Nike logo in 1964 for a fee of $35 dollars. *They paid her mostly in experience. Now she knows not to work with Nike.*

❯ Noel Botham, *The Mega Book of Useless Information* (John Blake, 2009), 264.

Only 37 percent of Americans have a passport. *The noble minority; it's up to you to spread the American gospel of obesity and mediocrity to the rest of the world.*

❯ "Passport Statistics," U.S. Department of State, *www.travel.state.gov.*

The average American spends about a year of his or her life watching television commercials. *Think of all that wasted time when you could have been masturbating.*

❯ Erin Barrett and Jack Mingo, *Random Kinds Of Factness: 1001 (or So) Absolutely True Tidbits About (Mostly) Everything* (Conari Press, 2005), 2.

Because it was discovered in Alabama, the element astatine was originally called "alabamine." *To date, the most interesting thing to ever happen in Alabama.*

❯ Glen Vecchione, Joel Harris, and Sharon Harris, *A Little Giant Book: Science Facts* (Sterling, 2007), 73.

One out of four Americans relies on a personal septic system instead of a public sewage system. *Translation: twenty-five percent of American homes are full of shit.*

❯ "Septic Systems," National Environmental Services Center, *www.nesc.wvu.edu.*

William Cosper of Childersburg, Alabama, has been struck by lightning on four separate occasions—twice while he was alive and twice after he died. His first tombstone was reduced to a pile of rubble shortly after his burial, and the replacement was later destroyed by yet another strike. *Universe 4: William Cosper: −4.*

❯ Mark Moran, Mark Sceurman, and Matt Lake, *Weird U.S. The ODDyssey Continues: Your Travel Guide to America's Local Legends and Best Kept Secrets* (Sterling, 2008), 336.

The average American child will witness 8,000 deaths on television before finishing elementary school. *Unless they watch the news, in which case it's double that.*

> "Television & Health," California State University–Northridge, *www.csun.edu.*

When viewed from space, there appears to be a massive city sitting in the middle of rural Nebraska. The illusion is due to light pollution from the Bakken oil field. *We love three things in America: food, oil, and more oil. And more food.*

> Ken Paulman, "The Bakken from Space," *Midwest Energy News*, November 14, 2011, *www.midwestenergynews.com.*

A 2009 study of American money found that as much as 95 percent of our paper currency contains trace amounts of cocaine. *We're almost there guys, just 5 percent more.*

> Christine Dell'Amore, "Cocaine on Money: Drug Found on 90% of U.S. Bills," *National Geographic*, August 16, 2009, *www.news.nationalgeographic.com.*

Botulism toxin, an ingredient used in the United States to perform Botox treatment, is the single most deadly poison on earth. Two kilograms of the substance is enough to kill every human on earth. *Well, do you want to get laid or do you want to not have the deadliest substance known to man injected into your face?*

> Loz Blain, "Genome Sequence of the World's Most Lethal Toxin," Gizmag, April 27, 2007, *www.gizmag.com.*

Of the more than 80,000 chemicals used in the United States, only about 300 have ever undergone health and safety testing. *Well, most of us are still alive. That's got to count for something.*

> David Biello, "Robot Allows High-Speed Testing of Chemicals," *Scientific American*, October 13, 2011, *www.scientificamerican.com*.

Each year, about 10 percent of the salt mined throughout the world is used to de-ice America's roads and highways. *What was once one of the most precious substances known to man, we now toss on our streets. Yay, America!*

> Glen Vecchione, Joel Harris, and Sharon Harris, *A Little Giant Book: Science Facts* (Sterling, 2007), 73.

In 2011, a group of researchers at Kimberly-Clark Professional sought out the filthiest surfaces in America. Gas pump handles topped the list, with public mailboxes and escalator rails coming in a close second. *What were you saying about New Jersey's "stupid" no-pump laws?*

> "Gas Pump Handles Top Study of Filthy Services," Reuters, October 25, 2011, *www.reuters.com*.

The first documented use of the word "nerd" was in *If I Ran the Zoo*, a book written by Dr. Seuss. *"Lorax," as everyone knows, was an ancient Egyptian word for "hippie."*

> "How Dr. Seuss Invented Nerds," Geek.com, *www.geek.com*.

Known as the "Boogeyman," serial killer Albert Fish stalked the East Coast in the early twentieth century, abducting and killing young children and even cannibalizing some of his victims. While he claimed to have killed more than 100 children, he was convicted and put to death solely for the death of ten-year-old Grace Budd. *If he killed all 100 at once, it could have been self defense. Eight-year-olds are dangerous en masse.*

❯ "The Werewolf of Wisteria," *Crime* magazine, August 1, 2011, *www.crimemagazine.com.*

After Albert Fish's capture, doctors discovered he had a habit of inflicting harm on himself in strange ways. X-rays revealed he had twenty-nine needles inserted into his groin that he had been unable to remove himself. *One word: magnets.*

❯ Marilyn Bardsley, "Albert Fish," Tru TV, *www.trutv.com.*

Eighty-five percent of serial killers come from the United States.
We take our desire to be the best at everything very seriously here.

❯ "Mook Examines Celebrity and Serial Killers," About.com, *www.crime.about.com.*

The Mormon Church maintains an entire website devoted solely to what types of underwear are appropriate. *When in doubt, just go with nothing.*

❯ "Frequently Asked Questions," Mormon Underwear, *www.mormon-underwear.com*.

In 1962, a devastating fire broke out in a series of coal mines beneath the town of Centralia, Pennsylvania, and the inferno has raged on ever since. Scientists speculate there is enough coal to fuel the flames for another 250 years. *Whether it's 250 years or 250 days, I don't think anybody's dying to move back to Centralia, Pennsylvania, anytime soon.*

❯ Kevin Krajick, "Fire in the Hole," *Smithsonian* magazine, May 2005, *www.smithsonianmag.com*.

A monster truck burns between two and three gallons of methanol per 250-foot run. *Worth every penny.*

❯ Noel Botham, *The Mega Book of Useless Information* (John Blake, 2009). 199.

Although the rule was rarely enforced, longhaired men were not permitted in the Disneyland park until the 1960s. *You could always just pretend to be an ugly woman though.*

❯ Dane Sherwood, Sandy Wood, and Kara Kovalchik, *The Pocket Idiot's Guide to Not So Useless Facts* (Penguin Group, 2006), 55.

ABOUT THE AUTHOR

Eric Grzymkowski is a humor writer and amateur trivia expert. When not writing, he can be found shouting out the answers to *Jeopardy!* questions and increasing his knowledge base by aimlessly surfing the Internet. He frequents bar trivia nights and one time almost won. Almost. He lives in Cambridge, MA.